AAKER ON BRANDING

"No enterprise can be successful today without embracing the principles articulated so clearly by Professor Aaker. This is the ultimate *"tour de force"* of his collective genius in the critical discipline of brand management."

—**Joseph V. Tripodi**, Chief Marketing and
Commercial Officer, Coca-Cola

"David's new book is for learners and experts alike – a knowledge center for branding principles and strategies every marketer needs to know and practice. Why go anywhere else?"

—**Elisa Steele**, CMO Consumer Apps and Service, Microsoft

Also by David Aaker

Consumerism: Search for the Consumer Interest 4th Edition
(co-edited with George Day)

Multivariate Analysis in Marketing: Theory and Applications
2nd Edition (editor)

Advertising Management 5th Edition
(with Rajeev Batra and John Myers)

Marketing Research 11th Edition
(with V Kumar, Robert Leone, and George Day)

Strategic Market Management 10th Edition

Managing Brand Equity

Brand Equity and Advertising (edited with Alex Biel)

Building Strong Brands

Brand Leadership (with Erich Joachimsthaler)

Brand Portfolio Strategy

From Fargo to the World of Brands: My Story So Far

Spanning Silos: The New CMO Imperative

Brand Relevance: Making Competitors Irrelevant

Three Threats to Brand Relevance: Strategies that Work. (e-book)

AAKER ON BRANDING

20 Principles That Drive Success

DAVID AAKER

NEW YORK

AAKER ON BRANDING

20 Principles That Drive Success

Published in New York, New York, by Morgan James Publishing. Morgan James and The Entrepreneurial Publisher are trademarks of Morgan James, LLC. www.MorganJamesPublishing.com

The Morgan James Speakers Group can bring authors to your live event. For more information or to book an event visit The Morgan James Speakers Group at www.TheMorganJamesSpeakersGroup.com.

ISBN 978-1-61448-832-3 paperback
ISBN 978-1-61448-833-0 eBook
ISBN 978-1-61448-834-7 audio
ISBN 978-1-61448-870-5 hardcover
Library of Congress Control Number: 2013945748

BitLit

FOR ALL THE BOOKS YOU OWN

FREE eBook edition for your existing eReader with purchase

_____

PRINT NAME ABOVE

For more information, instructions, restrictions, and to register your copy, go to **www.bitlit.ca/readers/register** or use your QR Reader to scan the barcode:

Cover Design by:
Paul Wang

Chris Treccani
www.3dogdesign.net

Interior Design by:
Bonnie Bushman
bonnie@caboodlegraphics.com

In an effort to support local communities, raise awareness and funds, Morgan James Publishing donates a percentage of all book sales for the life of each book to Habitat for Humanity Peninsula and Greater Williamsburg.

Get involved today, visit
www.MorganJamesBuilds.com

Habitat for Humanity®
Peninsula and
Greater Williamsburg
Building Partner

To my wife Kay and
my daughters Jennifer, Jan, and Jolyn and their families.
They all support and inspire.

TABLE OF CONTENTS

Introduction:

WHY THIS BOOK?

What is a brand? Far more than a name and logo, it is an organization's promise to a customer to deliver what the brand stands for not only in terms of functional benefits but also emotional, self-expressive, and social benefits. But a brand is more than delivering on a promise. It is also a journey, an evolving relationship based on the perceptions and experiences that a customer has every time he or she connects to the brand.

Brands are powerful. They serve as the core of a customer relationship, a platform for strategic options, and a force that affects financials, including stock return. Consider the most compelling brands and their brand "essences." Google is associated with competence and dominance in search engines and more, Harley-Davidson with emotional and self-expressive benefits, IBM with competent solutions-oriented computer services, Singapore Airlines with special service, Mercedes for those who appreciate the best, American Express with incredible customer satisfaction and ability to connect through digital programs, and Patagonia with sustainability. The strength of these brands has led to customer loyalty, business success, resilience despite product problems, and the basis for moving into new products or markets.

1

Additionally, brands and brand strategy are simply fun and interesting. Many a time has a CEO allocated half an hour to a brand strategy session and end up staying for hours affirming on their way out that the session was the most fun time working in months. It is fascinating to know what brand positions succeed, what brand-building programs get traction, how a brand is successfully leveraged into new markets, and so on. The creativity and diversity in brand strategy can be an endless source of conversation.

One objective of this book is to provide an extremely compact presentation of several dozen of the most useful branding concepts and practices organized into the "20" essential principles of branding. These principles provide a broad understanding of brands, brand strategy, brand portfolios, and brand building that all business, marketing, and brand strategists should know. This exposition of branding principles should be useful for those who would like a refresh as well as for those who lack a background in branding and would like to get up to speed quickly.

A second objective is to provide a roadmap to the creation, enhancement, and leverage of strong brands. What are the steps needed to create strong brands? What are the options along the way? How does a strategist move a brand or brand family to the next level to become a source of strength rather than a strategy drag? Whatever the business, it is crucial to understand how to establish a brand vision (also termed brand identity), implement that vision, keep a brand strong in the face of aggressive competitors and dynamic markets, leverage the resulting brand strength, and effectively manage the brand portfolio so it delivers synergy, clarity, and leverage.

Branding is complex and idiosyncratic. Every context is different. In short, all twenty principles will not apply in every setting, but will provide a check list of strategies, perspectives, tools, and concepts that represent not only what you should know, but also various action options to consider. These principles will enhance the objective of creating and maintaining strong, enduring brands and coherent brand families that will support business strategies going forward.

The twenty principles describe concepts and practices drawn in part from my last eight books. Six of these books are on branding—*Managing Brand Equity, Building Strong Brands, Brand Leadership* (with Erich Joachimsthaler), *Brand Portfolio Strategy, Brand Relevance: Making Competitors Irrelevan*t, and *Three Threats to Brand Relevance*. The other two, *Spanning Silos* and *Strategic Market Management 10th* *edition*, cover closely related areas. The principles also draw on my other writings; in particular, the weekly davidaaker.com blog initiated in the fall of 2010, my blog posts on HBR.org, my columns in the AMA's *Marketing News* and in Germany's *absatzwirtschaft*, and in articles in the *California Management Review, Harvard Business Review, Journal of Brand Strategy, Market Leader*, and elsewhere.

The book is designed to consolidate the larger literature of the branding field and to efficiently teach or review the best branding practices. At more than 2,300 pages, my eight books alone are a bit overwhelming. Add to that the dozens of other brand books on the shelves and the several journals devoted to branding and you're in for some serious information overload. It is hard to know what to read and which concepts to adapt. As with anything, a lot of good ideas are out there competing with some that are inferior, need updating, or are subject to misinterpretation or misapplication. There are also ideas that, while plausible, are simply wrong (if not dangerous) especially if taken literally.

The chapters in this book do not have to be read in order, although the first two are worth reviewing first as they are so basic to the concept of strategic branding. After that, you might flip through the remaining chapters and identify those that relate to current pain points. Or look for chapters that intrigue or seem provocative and may be a possible source of new perspectives.

Here is how I divided the book thematically:

Part 1: Recognize that brands are assets with strategic value. The breakthrough idea that changed marketing over two decades ago is that brands are strategic assets. Brands are platforms for future success and create ongoing value for the organization. Thus, brand building is strategic, very different than tactical efforts to stimulate sales

Part 2. Have a compelling brand vision that guides and inspires. A brand vision should attempt to go beyond functional benefits to consider organizational values; a higher purpose; brand personality; and emotional, social, and self-expressive benefits. Look for opportunities to create and own innovations that customers "must have" and to position categories and subcategories as well as brands.

Part 3. Bring the brand vision to life. Create initiatives and brand-building programs that support the brand. Look to customer sweet spots—areas customers are interested if not passionate about—and develop programs around them with the brand as partner. Let digital programs lead or amplify. Strive for brand vision and brand execution consistency over time. Develop rich, strong internal branding connected to the values and culture of the organization in part through stories.

Part 4. Maintain relevance. Recognize and respond to the three threats to relevance and learn how to energize the brand.

Part 5: Manage and leverage the brand portfolio. Create a strategy that identifies brand roles (such as strategic brands or endorser brands), leverage the brand into new product arenas, analyze the risks and options of vertical brand extensions, and manage silo organizational units, where the brand spans products and countries.

THE BOTTOM LINE

A brand will benefit if it can develop an actionable higher purpose. This book, like my other brand books, also has a higher purpose. It is intended to advance the theory of branding and the practice of brand management and, by extension, the practice of business and organizational management. The purpose is to give marketing strategists a counter weight to the dominance of short-term financials in managing businesses. There should be a drive to build strategic brand assets that will provide the platforms for future success. This book will hopefully provide a role in that quest.

PART I

Recognize That Brands Are Assets

Chapter 1

BRANDS ARE ASSETS THAT DRIVE STRATEGY

A brand is the face of a business strategy.
—**Prophet dictum**

Sometime in the late 1980s, an explosive idea emerged, the idea that brands are assets, have equity, and drive business strategy and performance.

Conceiving of brands as assets started a dramatic and far-reaching cascade of change. It altered perceptions of marketing and brand management, how brands are managed and measured, and the role of marketing executives. Those firms that adopted and successfully implemented this view saw brand building shift from a tactical effort that could be safely delegated to a communication team to a driver of business strategy.

It was an idea whose time was right. A critical mass of executives believed that key brands in their portfolio were inadequate in vision or strength to support the business strategy, but they no longer looked at tweaking communication tactics as the solution. Unless there were brand assets that enabled the business strategy and resonated

7

with the customers, the strategy was all but doomed. That view was particularly clear for executives who were managing a strategy change. The net result? More and more executives realized that tactical brand management was inadequate and a strategy-led brand vision, plus organizational processes and skills to implement that vision, was critically needed.

The acceptance of the "brand as asset" concept was enhanced by the fact that the prevailing belief—that brand marketing's prime role was to stimulate sales—had failed in many contexts. In packaged goods, there was the disastrous experience in the early 1980s stimulated by the advent of scanner-based, real-time data. This data enabled experiments that clearly showed that price promotions such as 20 percent off or two-for-one were incredibly effective at generating sales. The natural outcome was a huge spurt in price programs which taught consumers to wait for the next deal and avoid buying at the regular price. As a result, price became the important purchase driver and brand differentiation fell. Brands like Kraft took years to recover their equity and loyal customer base.

Executives also saw that brand assets were needed to create top-line growth which became an imperative for many firms because cost-reduction programs had past the point of diminishing returns and lost their ability to materially affect profitability. The most effective path to growth, to create an innovative new offering, required the ability to develop a new brand or adapt an existing one to support the new offering. Further, brand-extension strategies, extending an existing master brand into new products or into value or super-premium segments, was viable only if the brand assets were developed and managed strategically with future extension options in mind.

The brand-as-asset view had both face validity and quantitative support. Face validity came from a realization that, especially in service and BtoB contexts, customers were making buy decisions and appraising their use experience on brand elements that went beyond price and functional attributes. Quantitative support was based on data-based efforts that showed that brands *did* have substantial asset value and made the new paradigm palatable to the CFOs and CEOs of the world.

The academic world played a role in the elevation of brands to strategic status as well, stimulated by the influential 1988 brand conference hosted by Marketing Science Institute (MSI), a consortium of firms that both funds and guides academic research. The conference provided an outlet for top marketing executives to signify the need to elevate brand to a strategic level. After this conference, brand equity research vaulted to the number one academic research priority. Academic research in brand extension decisions, quantifying the impact of brands on financial performance, refining relevant tools such as brand personality measurement, and conceptualizing brand equity was accelerated.

It was a perfect storm of ideas and timing. However, the surge of interest and organizational change did not immediately impact all industries and firms. Many firms were slow to join the parade, particularly those in which marketing strengths were not in evidence and/or those that were highly decentralized. One barrier, in addition to buying into the message, was the difficulty of actual implementation. However, the willingness of firms to adopt the brand-as-asset view and, as important, their ability to implement the new perspective, has grown steadily over time, proving this is not some management fad.

The implications were and are extraordinary.

FROM TACTICAL TO STRATEGIC

One paradigm, once dominant, posits brand management as tactical. Brand management is something that can be delegated in part to an advertising manager or agency because it is mostly about managing the image, creating an advertising campaign, managing a distribution strategy, developing sales promotions, supporting the sales force, getting packaging right and other such tasks.

When brands are considered assets, the role of brand management radically changes, from tactical and reactive to strategic and visionary. A strategic brand vision linked to both the current and future business strategies and providing a guidepost for future offerings and marketing programs becomes imperative. Brand management also becomes broader, encompassing issues like strategic market insights, the stimulation of "big" innovations, growth strategies, brand portfolio strategies, and global brand strategies.

THE MARKETING ROLE IS ELEVATED

With a strategic view, the brand needs to be managed by people higher in the organization, often the top marketing professional in the business organization and his or her executive colleagues. For marketing-driven organizations, where there is marketing talent at the top, the ultimate brand champion will be a top executive, perhaps the CEO. When the brand represents the organization, as it often does in a BtoB or service firm, the CEO often is involved in bringing the brand to life because, in that case, the brand is intertwined with the organizational culture and values as well as its business strategy.

Marketing now gets a seat at the strategy table, a participant at creating and managing the business strategy. The elevation of brands and brand building as a driver of business strategy provides a point of entry for the marketing team. Once in place, marketing has much to offer to business strategy development starting with customer insights that can and should enable growth initiatives and be the basis for strategic resource allocation. Further, the very heart of business strategy is market segmentation and the customer value proposition, the prospects of which will be informed by the marketing team.

FOCUS ON BRAND EQUITY

Shifting the emphasis from tactical measures, such as short-term sales, to strategic measures of brand equity and other indicators of long-term financial performance is a monumental change. The guiding premise is that strong brands can be the basis of competitive advantage and long-term profitability going forward. A primary brand-building goal will be to build, enhance, or leverage brand equity, the major dimensions of which are—awareness, associations, and loyalty of the customer base.

- **Brand awareness**, an often-undervalued asset, has been shown to affect perceptions, liking, and even behavior. People like the familiar and are prepared to ascribe all sorts of positive attributes to items they find familiar. Further, brand awareness can be a signal of success, commitment, and substance, attributes that can be critical to industrial buyers of big-ticket items and consumer buyers of durables. The logic is that if a brand is recognized, there must be a reason. Finally, awareness can affect whether a brand is recalled at a key time in the purchasing process and thus among the brands the customer considers.

- **Brand associations** include product attributes (Crest, Volvo), design (Calvin Klein, Apple), social programs (Avon, Patagonia), quality (Lexus, Southwest Airlines), user imagery (Mercedes, Nike), product breadth (Amazon, Marriott), being global (VISA, Ford), innovation (3M, Virgin), systems solutions (IBM, Salesforce.com), brand personality (MetLife, Singapore Airlines), and symbols (Tiffany blue box, Golden Arches).... anything that connects the customer to the brand. They can be the basis for a customer relationship, purchase decision, use experience, and brand loyalty. A critical part of managing brands as assets involves determining what associations to develop, creating programs that will enhance those associations, and linking them to the brand.
- **Brand loyalty** is at the heart of any brand's value because once obtained, loyalty is persistent. Customer inertia will benefit the brand that has earned loyalty. Breaking a loyalty link is difficult and expensive for a competitor. As such, one brand-building goal is to strengthen the size and intensity of each loyalty segment by making the basis of the customer relationship consistent over time and, whenever possible, rich, deep, and meaningful.

FROM BRANDS TO BRAND FAMILIES

Brand management has historically been about focusing on a single brand and country as if it was operating in isolation within the firm and the world market. That approach is a legacy of the classic P&G brand management system that can be traced to a 1931 memo with a job description for a "brand man" written by Neil McElroy, then a P&G junior marketing manager who later became CEO and then Secretary of Defense, who was struggling to manage a Camay soap brand that was overshadowed by the Ivory soap brand. The premise was that each brand was autonomous, with its own brand program, a view that is no longer strategically viable.

More and more organizations are realizing that strategic brand management has to involve a "family" of brands, managed as a portfolio. The essence of brand portfolio strategy is to make sure the brands of the organization, including subbrands, endorsers, and branded innovations, work in concert to create clarity and synergy, cooperating instead of competing. Each brand needs a well-defined role, which might actually include helping other brands. And these roles could change over time, as can the product scope, as a brand is extended both horizontally and vertically. Firms are finding ways to allocate resources over brands and markets to protect the brand stars of the future and to make sure each brand has the resources to be successful in its current *and* future assigned roles.

STRATEGIC ISSUES OF BRAND EXTENSIONS

When brand is viewed as an asset, the opportunity arises to leverage that asset to generate growth, an objective of most firms. It can be used as a master brand or perhaps as an endorser to support a strategic entry into another product class, providing a platform that will deliver awareness and positive associations such as perceived quality. A brand can also be leveraged vertically to support an upscale or downscale offering. However, under the "brand as asset" model the goal is not just to create a successful brand extension but to enhance the brand and the whole brand portfolio. A strategic, broader perspective is introduced.

ORGANIZATIONAL SILO ISSUES NEED TO BE ADDRESSED

Nearly all brands span different silo organizations defined by products, markets, or countries. At some firms (GE or Toshiba, for example), a brand could drive customer relationships in a thousand product markets. When brands are viewed tactically, silo autonomy appears to work as it allows those organizational units closest to the customer to adapt the brand to their needs.

However, losing control over silo brand-building creates inefficiencies, lost opportunities, and diminution of the brand. When the brand is allowed to be taken in different directions by different silos, it will become confused and weak. Further, effective and efficient brand building often requires scale and the motivation to share best practices. As a result of these issues and others, it has become clear that centralized coordination is needed across the countries and products that are using the brand to drive the business.

BRAND MANAGER AS COMMUNICATION TEAM LEADER

In the old days, the brand manager often just acted as the coordinator and scheduler of tactical communication programs. It was a simpler time, with a limited number of media levers to pull and a simpler charge: generate sales.

Brand builders now face a very different world, a world with a set of communication vehicles that are numerous, complex, and dynamic. Creating and managing an integrated communication program (IMC) is much tougher. Further, the communication task now has a charge beyond sales generation; it needs to build brand assets guided by a clear brand vision in part by strengthening brand associations and customer relationships. Not easy. And the task is made more difficult as increasingly a master brand is spread over products and countries, raising difficult budget allocation decisions.

The brand-as-asset driven communication needs to also generate understanding and buy-in inside the organization, because the brand will only deliver on the brand promise if the employees "believe" and live the brand in all the customer touchpoints. The need is thus to build the brand internally as well as externally.

WHY IS IT HARD?

Why has such a compelling concept been slow to be accepted? And why is it slow to be implemented even when accepted? Three main reasons:

First, the power of short-term financials is overwhelming. Managers look to these measures for evaluation in part because there is instant gratification in seeing immediate results of actions and programs. Further, finance theory has "proven" that the role of business is to maximize stock return and the reality is that stock return responds to short-term earnings changes because alternative measures are either unavailable or unreliable. As a result, managers learn that careers advance when they deliver short-term improvements in financials.

Second, building brand assets is no easy feat. Getting the brand vision right and then finding breakthrough ways to bring it to life ranges from difficult to impossible. And if the payoff is three to five years out, it is hard to convince executives that the performance is on track when the short-term financials are flat or declining, in part because convincing surrogates for long-term performance are hard to generate. As a result, even organizations that believe can find it hard to deliver.

Third, some organizations do not have a marketing capability in the form of people, processes, or culture, and therefore will be slow to accept the brand-as-asset view. This is more likely for organizations in BtoB or high-tech settings and for firms in countries like China, which have operated under the protection of a government and are focused on manufacturing and distribution rather than on brands. Executives in such environments are slow to accept the strategic quality of brands and find it difficult to allocate resources in that direction.

THE BOTTOM LINE

It is hard to overemphasize the importance of the brand-as-asset concept. In the history of marketing there are a few concepts that have truly transformed the practice of marketing. Mass marketing, the marketing concept, and segmentation would surely be named. But the "brand as asset" view of brands and brand building, although not always easy to implement, needs to be on the list as well.

Chapter 2

BRAND ASSETS HAVE REAL VALUE

Brand value is very much like an onion. It has layers and a core.
The core is the user who will stick with you until the very end.
—**Edwin Artzt**, former CEO P&G

B rand assets have real value. This assertion is critical to living in the new brand-as-asset world, with all its implications, from business strategy to marketing programs to the resourcing and management of brand building. But as branding becomes strategic and earns a seat at the executive table, the CEOs and CFOs of the world, who may have sympathy with the brand asset concept, will ultimately need proof that value actually exists. A conceptual argument will be part of the persuasion, but more empirical evidence may be necessary as well.

Investments in brand were easy to justify under the classic brand management paradigm, which focused on short-term sales. Brand programs either delivered immediate sales and profits or they did not. Building brand assets, however, may involve consistent reinforcement over years and only a small portion of the pay-off may occur immediately—in fact, in the short run brand building may depress profits. So the need is to measure long-term brand impacts or its surrogates. We have left the tactical world, in which short-term measures work.

There are a variety of ways that brand asset value can be demonstrated, including case studies, brand valuations, quantitative studies of the impact of brand equity, and the role of brand assets in conceptual business strategy models.

CASE STUDIES

A vivid, convincing, and memorable way to demonstrate brand asset value is to look at case studies. Look to brands that have undeniably contributed to the creation of enormous value. The Apple brand, for example, with its creative, independent personality and reputation for being a leading innovator, is a driver of one of the most valuable firms in the world. BMW has gotten traction in large part because of a brand defined around the "ultimate driving machine" and the self-expressive benefits that the badge lends to the driver. Trader Joe's has dominated a subcategory with a brand that has crystalized a set of values and life-style that delivers both self-expressive and social benefits.

Consider also the value of creating a brand that is so strong it can survive business blunders that sometimes undercut the brand promise. Such brands can lead a come-back that otherwise would be infeasible. Apple had a down period in its product line and business performance before Steve Jobs returned in 1997, but its brand allowed the business to come back when the product problems were remedied and innovation returned. The same can be said about Harley-Davidson, which went through a period of quality problems and saw the brand lead the business back once those problems were resolved. AT&T, the leading communication brand for three generations prior to the 1980s, spent almost two decades shouting price and fighting service issues, and yet today it is still one of the strongest and most relevant brands in its category. These stories testify to the resilience and asset value of a strong brand.

Consider finally those brands that *did* collapse when managed badly, thereby losing enormous enterprise value. In the mid-1970s, Schlitz, the "Gusto" beer, was a close number two behind Budweiser when the firm decided to cut costs by using a yeast-centered brewing process, which cut the processing time from twelve to four days, and by replacing barley malt with corn syrup.[1] Blind taste tests showed that the taste did not change. However, competitors were only too glad to talk about Schlitzes' efforts to reduce costs. Their suggestion that Schlitz had compromised quality became very real when it turned out that the beer, after sitting on the self, would turn cloudy and lose carbonation. Schlitz returned to its old production method and ran blind taste tests during the Super Bowl to prove the quality was back, but customers had lost confidence in the brand and the thought of finding "gusto" by drinking Schlitz became a joke. The brand damage led to its virtual disappearance from the market and caused the business to lose more than one billion dollars in value. This story, and others like it, shows that even strong brands can be vulnerable to decisions insensitive to the brand promise and customer relationships.

THE ASSET VALUE OF A BRAND

Another approach to demonstrate the asset value of a brand is to directly estimate the value of its equity. There is a logical process that yields an estimate of a brand's asset value, which can be helpful in demonstrating that brands are indeed assets and in showing how those brand assets are dispersed around the product-markets in which the firm is engaged.

Estimating the value of a brand starts with estimating the value of the product-market business units driven by the brand. The Ford Focus business in the United States, for example, would be evaluated by discounting its future expected earnings flow. The value of tangible assets (using either book or market value) is subtracted. The balance is due to intangible assets like manufacturing skill, people, R&D capability, and brand. These intangible assets are then subjectively allocated to brand and others. The key estimated number is the percent of the impact of the intangible assets that are due to brand power. This estimate can be done by a group of knowledgeable people within the firm working together or by themselves taking into account the business model and any information about the brand in terms of its relative awareness, associations, and customer loyalty. There might be disagreement as to whether a brand's role is 20 percent or 30 percent but there are rarely arguments about whether it should be 10 percent or 50 percent.

The value of the brand is then aggregated over countries to determine a value for the Ford Focus worldwide and then, finally, aggregated over the other Ford products to get an overall value of the Ford brand. This value can be cross-checked with the market cap of the Ford stock and the percentage of the Ford company sales that is driven by the Ford brand.

The value of brands throughout the world has been estimated annually by Interbrand, Millward Brown, and others for well over a decade. In 2013, there were seven brands valued by Interbrand over $40 billion (Apple, Google, Coca-Cola, IBM, Microsoft, GE, and McDonalds). The one-hundredth most valuable global brand was valued at over $80 million.

Although the estimate of the brand value as a percent of the value of its associated business is not reported, the Interbrand data of 2013 implies that the percentage varies from 10 to 25 percent (for brands like GE, Allianz, Accenture, Caterpillar, Hyundai, and Chevrolet) to 40 to 50 percent (for brands such as Google, Nike, and Disney) to over 60 percent for brands like Jack Daniel's, Coca-Cola, and Burberry).[2] Even 15 percent of the value of a business will usually represent an asset worth building and protecting; when it is much higher, the need to protect the brand-building budget becomes more compelling. A brand's estimated value can be an important statement about the wisdom and feasibility of creating brand assets.

It is tempting to use this measure to manage brands and brand building, but the reality is that it is too imprecise to play this role. The value will be driven by the stock market, competitor innovations, business strategy, product performance, and market dynamics that may have little to do with brand power and is based on several subjective parameter estimates that involve uncertainties and biases.

Brand value estimates can be worthwhile, however, in providing a frame of reference when developing brand-building programs and budgets. If a brand is worth $500 million, a budget of $5 million for brand building might be challenged as being too low. Or if $400 million of the brand's value was in Europe and $100 million in the United States, a decision to split evenly the brand-building budget may be questioned. Further, the process can add value by stimulating brand-management teams to think through exactly how their brand is working in the business strategy and what its components are. The insights gained will help enhance the business and brand strategy and the associated brand-building efforts.

PAYOFF FROM BRAND BUILDING PROGRAMS

Another approach to demonstrating brand value is to measure statistically the impact of brand equity changes on stock return, which is the ultimate measure of a long-term return on assets. In two studies I conducted with Professor Robert Jacobson of the University of Washington, we explored this relationship using time series data which included information on accounting-based earnings or return on investment (ROI) and models that sorted out the direction of causation.[3] The first data base from EquiTrend involved thirty-three brands representing publically traded firms like American Express, Chrysler, and Exxon; the second database, from Techtel, involved nine high tech firms including Apple, HP, and IBM.

Researchers in finance have shown a strong relationship between ROI changes and stock prices. On average, if ROI go up so, does a stock price. We found in both studies that the impact of increasing brand equity on stock return was nearly as great as ROI, 70 percent as much. Figure 1 presents the results of the EquiTrend study. The figure vividly shows that stock return responds to a large loss or large gain in brand equity, nearly as much as the response to ROI changes. In contrast, advertising, also tested in the study, had no impact on stock return except that which was captured by brand equity.

The brand equity to stock return relationship may be in part caused by the fact that brand equity supports a price premium that contributes to profitability. An analysis of the larger EquiTrend database has shown that brand equity is associated with a premium price. Thus, premium-priced brands like Mercedes, Levi, and Hallmark have substantial brand equity (as measured by perceived quality) advantages over competitors such as Buick, Lee Jeans, and American Greetings.

The high-tech study went on to examine the major brand equity changes that were observed. What causes the generally stable brand equity numbers to change? Some of the major changes were associated with significant product innovations (as opposed to incremental ones). But there was more. Major changes could also be attributed to visible product problems, change in top management, major lawsuit results, and competitor actions or fortunes that were notably successful or unsuccessful. The latter, of course, is usually out of the control of the brand's firm.

These studies show that when a real change in brand equity occurs, which is unlikely to happen with only advertising or promotions, there will be a substantial and measurable effect on stock return. Such a finding is persuasive evidence that brand equity will affect the real value of the business and the brand-as-asset model is valid.

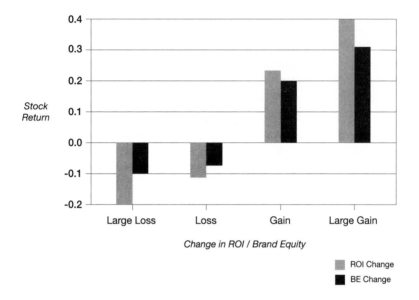

Change in ROI / Brand Equity

ROI Change
BE Change

The EquiTrend Study:
Stock Market Reaction to Changes
in Brand Equity and ROI
Figure 1

A CONCEPTUAL BUSINESS STRATEGY MODEL

The challenge facing those who would justify investments to build brand assets is similar to that facing those who would invest in any intangible. The three most important assets to most organization are people, information technology, and brands. All are intangible; they do not appear on the balance sheet. All add value to the organization that is difficult to quantify. The rationale for investment in any such intangible, therefore, must rest in part on a conceptual model of the business that affirms these intangibles represent key success factors underlying the business strategy.

One conceptual basis for brand investment is to contrast it with its strategic alternative, price competition. It is not a pretty picture.

Managers, especially those representing the number three or four brands, respond to excess capacity and price competition by lowering price. Competitors follow. Customers begin to focus more on price than on quality and differentiated features. Brands start resembling commodities, and firms begin to treat them as such. Profits erode.

The choice is between building brands or managing commodities. It does not take a strategic visionary to see that any slide toward commodity status should be resisted. Further, it is usually not inevitable. Consider the price premium paid for Morton's Salt (few products are more of a commodity than salt), Charles Schwab (a discount broker), or Emirates Airline. In each case, a strong brand has been able to resist pressures to focus on price. Management guru Tom Peters said it well: "In an increasingly crowded marketplace, fools will compete on price. Winners will find a way to create lasting value in the customer's mind."[4]

How should brand-building efforts be measured given that such programs will be expected to pay off over years and there are multiple drivers of success? The answer is to use measures of brand equity—awareness, key associations, and loyalty of a customer base. The relevance of these brand-equity measures requires a compelling conceptual business strategy model that shows that building brand strength is essential and will result in a competitive advantage that will pay off financially in the future.

SETTING AND ALLOCATING BRAND-BUILDING BUDGETS

The budget for any organizational intangible is difficult to create, allocate and defend. But some observations about the process can be made.

First, the role of a brand in the conceptual business strategy model needs to drive the budgeting process. What is its role and how crucial is the brand to the strategy? What are the strengths and weaknesses of the brand and where does the brand need to go? Is the priority to enhance awareness, create or change perceptions, or increase loyalty? How do the segments differ? What budget is likely to accomplish those tasks or at least give the strategy a chance to succeed?

Second, the quality of the communication program is much more important than the budget. One classic study found that quality of advertising (as measured by pre-post TV advertising exposure) was several times more able to explain variance in the market impact (as measured by sales gain) than the change in the advertising budget.[5] An implication is to spend more resources on creative ways to discover home-run ideas. It is possible or even likely that a $5 million budget behind a brilliant idea will be superior to a $20 million budget behind a mediocre idea. It is not just about spending money.

Third, measurement and experimentation can help. Experimenting with different brand-building ideas and budget levels takes a lot of the guesswork out of it. Beware, however, of using short-term sales to evaluate (although sometimes the absence of a short-term sales effect may signal a weak long-term effect). Using short-term sales as a criterion can lead to an over-emphasis on price deals, which can damage brands and thus long-term strategy. If running an experiment for a long time period is not feasible, measures of brand equity can be used as a surrogate for long-term market impact.

THE BOTTOM LINE

Brands are assets with strategic value. That assertion changes everything, but it needs to be communicated in a convincing way to motivate an organization to invest in brand building and in protecting brand assets. Case studies, brand-value estimates, and quantitative studies relating brand assets to stock return are reassuring, but the case still needs to be made in a specific context. That means developing conceptual models of the impact of brands on business strategy and by using "test and learn" experimentation.

PART II

Have a Compelling Brand Vision

Chapter 3

CREATE A BRAND VISION

Customers must recognize that you stand for something.
—**Howard Schultz**, Starbucks

Y ogi Berra, the fabled Yankee baseball player and manager, was said to have pointed out, "If you don't know where you are going, you'll end up somewhere else." That is so true about brands; you need to know where they are to end up.

Your brand needs to have a brand vision: an articulated description of the aspirational image for the brand; what you want the brand to stand for in the eyes of customers and other relevant groups like employees and partners. Brand vision (sometimes labeled brand identity or brand values or brand pillars) ultimately drives the brand-building component of the marketing program and greatly influences the rest. It should be one of the centerpieces of the strategic planning process. In prior books, I labeled it brand identity, but brand vision captures the strategic, aspirational nature of the concept and avoids confusion that is introduced because, for some, identity refers to the graphic design surrounding the brand.

When the brand vision clicks—is spot on—it will reflect and support the business strategy, differentiate from competitors, resonate with customers, energize and inspire the employees and partners, and precipitate a gush of ideas for marketing programs. When absent or superficial, the brand will drift aimlessly and marketing programs are likely to be inconsistent and ineffective.

The brand vision model is one structural framework for the development of a brand vision with a point of view that distinguishes it from others in several ways.[1]

First, a brand is more than a three-word phrase; it may be based on six to twelve vision elements. Most brands cannot be defined by a single thought or phrase, and the quest to find this magic brand concept can be fruitless or, worse, can leave the brand with an incomplete vision missing some relevant brand vision elements. The vision elements are prioritized into the two to five that are the most compelling and differentiating, termed the "core vision elements," while the others are labeled "extended vision elements." The core elements will reflect the value propositions going forward and drive the brand-building programs and initiatives.

Second, the extended vision elements provide a useful role. They add texture to the brand vision, allowing most strategists to make better judgments as to whether a program is "on brand." The extended vision affords a home for important aspects of the brand, such as a brand personality, that may not merit being a core vision element, and for elements, such as high quality, that are crucial for success but may not be a basis for differentiation. Such elements can and should influence branding programs. Too often during the process of creating a brand vision, a person's nominee for an aspiration brand association is dismissed because it could not be a centerpiece of the brand. When such an idea can be placed in the extended vision, the discussion can go forward. An extended vision element sometimes evolves into a core element, and without staying visible throughout the process that would not happen.

Third, the brand vision model is not a "one size fits all, fill in the box" model with pre-specified dimensions, where all brands in all contexts need to fill in each box even if the box does not apply to them. Nor are brands excluded from using a dimension that lacks a "box." Rather, the dimensions are selected that are relevant for the context at hand. And contexts vary. Organizational values and programs are likely to be important for service and BtoB firms but not for consumer package goods. Innovation is likely to be important for high-tech brands but less so for some packaged goods brands. Personality is often more important for durables and less so for corporate brands. The dimensions that are employed will be a function of the marketplace, the strategy, the competition, the customers, the organization, and the brand.

Fourth, the brand vision is aspirational and can differ from the current image. It is the associations the brand needs to have going forward, given its current and future business strategy. Too often a brand executive feels constrained and uncomfortable going beyond what the brand currently has permission to do. Yet most brands need to improve on some dimensions to compete, and add new dimensions in order to create new growth platforms. A brand that has plans to extend to a new category, for example, will probably need to go beyond the current image.

Fifth, the brand essence represents a central theme of the brand vision and is optional. When the right brand essence is found, it can be magic in terms of internal communication, inspiration to employees and partners, and guiding programs. Consider "Transforming Futures," the brand essence of the London School of Business, "Ideas for Life" for Panasonic, or "Family Magic" for Disneyland. In each case, the essence provides an umbrella over what the brand aspires to do. The essence should always be sought. However, there are times in which it actually gets in the way and is better omitted. One BtoB brand, Mobil (now ExxonMobil), had leadership, partnership, and trust as the core brand elements. Forcing an essence on this brand would likely be awkward. If the essence does not fit or is not compelling, it will soak up all the energy in the room. In these cases, the core vision elements are better brand drivers.

Sixth, the brand position is a short-term communication guide that often expresses what will be communicated to what target audience with what logic. The current positioning often emphasizes the brand vision elements that will appeal and are now credible and deliverable. As organizational capabilities and programs emerge or as markets change, the positioning message might evolve or change. The centerpiece of the position is often a tagline communicated externally, that need not and usually does not correspond to the brand essence, which is an internally communicated concept.

THE PROCESS

The brand vision development process starts with context and strategy. An in-depth analysis of customer segments, competitors, market trends, environmental forces, the current brand strengths and weaknesses, and the business strategy going forward is required background. The business strategy, which includes the product-market investment plan, the value propositions, the assets and skills that will support, and the functional plan, is necessary because the brand strategy is both driven by and an enabler of the business strategy. If the business strategy is vague or nonexistent, it often will have to be developed or articulated as part of the brand vision development.

The second step is to identify all aspirational associations. These items, which are often from fifty to a hundred in quantity, are then grouped, and each group is given a label. This grouping and labeling aspect is crucial and difficult. It can take weeks to get the right grouping and find just the right set of labels.

Associations can take many forms including attributes, functional benefits, applications, user imagery, brand personality, organizational programs and values, and self-expressive, emotional, or social benefits. They should each resonate with customers, really matter to them, and reflect and support the business strategy going forward.

Associations should also provide a point of differentiation that supports the value proposition or represent a point of parity. Although gaining differentiation, hopefully with some "must haves," is important, achieving parity on a key dimension for which a competitor has a meaningful advantage can be decisive in gaining relevance and market success. The parity goal is to be perceived as "good enough" so that customers do not exclude your brand from consideration. In Chapter 15, gaining parity is shown to be one way to counter a relevance threat posed by being inadequate on a dimension.

A vision should be inspiring to the firm's employees and partners. It should make them care. Chapter 5, on organizational values, shows how a higher purpose can help, and Chapter 14, on internal branding, discusses how stories can bring a higher purpose to life. Additionally, an exceptional brand vision will precipitate brand-building ideas; in fact, they should just spill out. A vision in which brand-building programs are not apparent needs more work.

Ajax, for example, is a global service company created from a set of a half-dozen acquisitions, each of which continued to operate somewhat autonomously. It was becoming clear, though, that customers preferred a single-solution firm with broad capabilities. The new Ajax strategy was to orient its service to broad customer solutions and to get its operating units to work together seamlessly. The strategy represented a significant change in culture and operations. With respect to the brand vision, the elements "Partner with Customers," "Customized Solutions," "Collaborative," and "Close to Customers" were clustered and given the name Team Solutions, which became one of eight vision elements as shown in Figure 2. The brand goal was to provide a face to customers that matched this new strategy.

The third step is to prioritize the brand vision elements. The most important and potentially most impactful, the core vision elements, will be the primary drivers of the brand-building programs. For Ajax, the core vision included the "Spirit of Excellence," "Technology That Fits," as well as "Team Solutions." The remaining five vision elements make up the extended vision.

THE BERKELEY-HAAS SCHOOL OF BUSINESS BRAND VISION

The Berkeley-Haas School of Business created a brand vision that stimulated extensive changes in the school, helping them to refine the student body, the faculty, the research programs, and the curriculum. The four core brand vision elements are:[2]

- **Question the Status Quo.** "We lead by championing bold ideas, taking intelligent risks, and accepting sensible failures. This means speaking our minds even while it challenges convention. We thrive at the world's epicenter of innovation." Captures the aspiration of big ideas and the vitality of the innovation process.
- **Confidence without Attitude.** "We made decisions based on evidence and analysis, giving us the confidence to act without arrogance. We lead through trust and collaboration." Highly differentiating.
- **Students Always.** "We are a community designed for curiosity and the lifelong pursuit of personal and intellectual growth. This is not a place for those who feel they have learned all they need to learn." Makes Berkeley-Haas relevant to alumni and executive programs.

- **Beyond Yourself.** "We shape our world by leading ethically and responsibly. As stewards of our enterprises, we take the longer view in our decisions and actions. This often means putting larger interests above our own." Describes a higher purpose.

The essence, which nicely captures the four core elements, is "We develop leaders who redefine how we do business." A different take on innovation and leadership, it aspires to redefine rather than simply refine the business.

The fourth step is to create a brand essence, a single thought that reflects the core of the brand vision. For Ajax, "Commitment to Excellence—Anytime, Anywhere, Whatever It Takes," as shown in Figure 2, was a punchy essence that captured for them their core identity.

The final step is the brand position, The brand position for Ajax involved a difficult decision around aspirational associations. Should Ajax position around team solutions even though the firm could not yet deliver? Being ahead of what is being delivered could serve to motivate the employees by signaling that the future business strategy depends on being able to deliver behind the aspirational promise. However, the more conservative option is to delay putting an aspirational association out as part of the positioning effort until it is credible, and until the firm has developed the ability to deliver on the promise…much safer to instead emphasize the other two core vision elements.

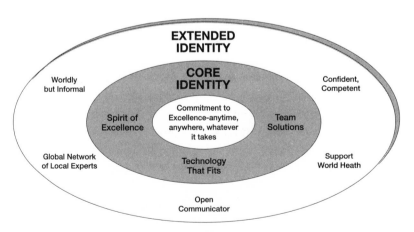

The Ajax Brand Vision
Figure 2

ADAPTING THE VISION

Having the same brand vision in all contexts has enormous advantages in coordinating brand efforts across product categories and markets, scaling brand-building programs, and gaining internal clarity for the brand. However, the goal should be strong brands everywhere, not the same brand everywhere, and adaptation is often helpful and sometimes necessary.

Brands often span products and markets that may represent important differences such as in a brand's market share position (VW is dominant in Germany but not in the UK), brand image (some brands are premium in one product or country and have a value image in another), customer motivations (P&G's Olay found that in India people wanted skin that was lighter looking rather that younger looking), distribution channels (ice cream is not sold in bulk in some countries but only on a stick or other single serving form), local heritage (cultural differences between France and Germany matter for some products), and competitor positions (a desirable position, such as being the chocolate that contains a glass of milk, might be preempted). If the differences warrant, the brand identity and/or position should be adapted.

The challenge is to allow adaptation without the process leading to anarchy, inconsistency, and uncoordinated marketing programs. The brand vision model, because of its richness and flexibility, is well suited to several adaptation strategies. The core elements can be selectively highlighted, interpreted differently, or augmented.

Emphasizing Different Elements of the Brand Vision

A brand that has a core vision of two to five items can selectively draw from this list to maximize its impact on the silo market. A major financial services company was developing a loan program eventually to be used in many of the countries in which they operated. The brand vision included "easy to work with," "bias to yes," "flexibility," and "speed." Qualitative research followed up with a quantitative concept test in three representative countries showed that the markets reacted very differently. In the United States, "easy to work with" and "bias to yes" were the most effective appeals. In an Eastern European country, "easy to work with" and "speed" were the most impactful while in a developed Asian country "flexible," "easy to work with," and "speed" were the winners. So countries could dial up different aspects of the vision even though the vision was the same.

Spinning the Brand Story for the Local Market

The same brand vision can be applied across organizational silos, but elements of it could be interpreted differently in different markets. A hotel's friendly, interactive style may look different in different countries. Or social responsibility could take on water conservation in one country and worker conditions in another. Or the innovation story by an appliance firm could focus on affordable, compact appliances in emerging markets and on computer-aided features for a more advanced market.

ChevronTexaco has a core brand vision that consists of four values—clean, safe, reliable, and high quality. The country and regional markets and the product groups hold workshops to adapt that brand vision to their context. One mechanism is to interpret the core elements in their marketplace. So what is quality in the context of a convenience store? Or in a lube business? As a result, the silo units get a degree of flexibility but within the confines of the overall brand strategy.

Augment with Additional Vision Elements

Another way to adapt is to add a vision element to the master brand vision in the silo context that will be relevant and even compelling but not inconsistent with the global brand.

ChevronTexaco, in addition to allowing the silos to interpret the brand vision elements, also allows the country or product silos to add one vision element to the four element already in the core vision. So the lube business could add "performance" and the Asian group could add "respectfully helpful." The result is a greater ability to link with the silo customer. In part, because the addition is made in the context of the brand strategy workshop, there is little chance that any element would be added that would be inconsistent with the brand.

The added association such as an attribute, benefit, or personality should be valued by the silo organization but not by the "rest of the world." One energy company had a well-defined brand that worked throughout the world. However, in a South American country, customers were used to being cheated at the pump and getting less than they paid for. An honest pump was a believable and relevant point of differentiation. What was added to the brand promise in that country was in no way inconsistent with the global brand promise but, rather, reinforced aspects of it such as trust.

With a country spanning silos, the brand could add a local or country flavor by infusing associations that connect with the culture and heritage of the country. A brand in the French market, for example, could use a local sponsorship of an arts program to link to the France culture. There can be a tension between being local and global but being both is very doable. Sony has long had the objective of being three things in each market—global, Japanese, and local— the best of all worlds.

STRATEGIC IMPERATIVES VS. PROOF POINTS

The brand vision implies a promise to customers and a commitment by the organization. It cannot be an exercise in wishful thinking but, rather, needs to have substance behind it. Every brand vision element should ultimately have proof points, capabilities, and programs in place that enable the organization to deliver the promise of each brand vision element and its associated value proposition. Proof points can be visible or behind the scenes. The visible proof points behind Nordstrom's claim of outstanding service are its return policy and its empowered staff. The employee compensation system, together with hiring and training programs, are proof points the customer doesn't see.

When proof points are weak or missing, a strategic imperative is needed. A strategic imperative is a strategic investment in an asset, skill, people, or program that is essential if the customer promise is to be delivered. Delivering on a strategic imperative might require significant investment or a change in culture.

Consider the following. For a regional bank brand that aspires to have a comprehensive customer relationship, a strategic imperative might be to equip each customer contact person with access to all of the customer's accounts with the bank. For a premium audio equipment brand that aspires to be a technological leader, strategic imperatives might include an expanded R&D program and improved manufacturing quality. For a value subbrand for a household cleaning product that wants to have a price advantage, a strategic imperative might be to develop a cost culture.

The strategic imperative represents a reality check, because it makes the critical "must do" investments visible and thus stimulates an assessment as to the feasibility of the brand strategy. Are the investment resources available? Is the commitment from the organization really there? Is the organization capable of responding to the strategic imperative? If the answer to any of these questions is no, then the organization is unable or unwilling to deliver behind the brand promise. The promise will then become an empty advertising slogan that at best will be a waste of resources and at worst create a brand liability instead of a brand asset.

For example, if the regional bank is not willing to invest the tens of millions of dollars necessary to create the database needed to allow appropriate customer interaction, then the relationship bank concept will need to be rethought. If the audio components firm is not willing to create innovative products and improve manufacturing quality, a high-end brand may be doomed. If the household cleaning product manufacturer is not willing or able to create a subunit with a real cost culture, then the value market may be a recipe for failure.

THE BOTTOM LINE

There needs to be a brand vision to provide direction, inspiration, and justification to the brand-building effort. The brand-vision model is multidimensional, has core and extended elements, includes an optional essence, is tailored to the brand's context, is aspirational, and can be adapted to different product markets. A key part of the process of developing a brand vision is to create labels for clusters of aspirational image elements. Identifying strategic imperatives can distinguish "wishful thinking" from realistic aspirations. The next six chapters discuss concepts that can be called on to populate a brand vision.

Chapter 4

A BRAND PERSONALITY CONNECTS

A brand that captures your mind gains behavior.
A brand that captures your heart gains commitment.
—**Scott Talgo** brand strategist

W hat is the worst thing you can say about a person? No personality? Who wants to spend time with someone who is so boring they're described as having no personality? Better to be a jerk; at least then you're interesting and memorable. Having a personality is equally helpful to brands.

Brand personality can be defined as the set of human characteristics associated with the brand. Psychologists and consumer researchers have shown conclusively that people often can and do treat objects, from pets to plants to brands, as if they were people, even giving them names. When brands are treated as people, perceptions and behavior are affected. In one study, individuals who were asked to think of creative uses for a brick and were exposed subliminally to an Apple logo instead of a IBM logo, generated more unique ideas. In the same study, subjects behaved more honestly after exposed to a Disney Channel logo vs. an E! Channel logo. The behavior difference in each case was attributed to the power of the personality of the brands.[1] Mere exposure to a brand logo prompted individuals to behave in ways consistent to the brand personality.

Not all brands have a personality, or at least a strong, distinctive personality. However, those brands that do have personality have a significant advantage; they are more likely to stand out from the crowd and have a message. Personality is an important dimension of brand equity because, like human personality, it is both differentiating and enduring. Once established, it will provide benefits (or harm) over a long time horizon. Creating or supporting a personality should be part of the brand vision discussion for sure.

BUILDING A BRAND— WHY A BRAND PERSONALITY?

In building a brand, the brand personality construct can help:

Represent and Communicate Functional Benefits

A brand personality can be a vehicle for representing and cueing functional benefits and brand attributes. It can be easier to create a personality that implies a functional benefit than to communicate directly and convincingly that a functional benefit exists. Further, it is harder to attack or copy a personality than a functional benefit, because a personality is based on many elements and usually has been established over time. It is not easily changed. Consider the following examples:

- MetLife, the insurance company, generated a personality represented by the Peanuts characters that provides a warm and humorous dimension to a firm that otherwise would be considered bureaucratic, profit seeking, and impersonal. The personality softens perceptions and makes the aspirational "caring and approachable" dimension come to life.
- The Hallmark-as-person is sincere, sentimental, warm, genuine, wholesome, and ageless as well as competent and imaginative. This personality says much about the Hallmark offerings.

- The Energizer brand, because of its name and its rabbit symbol, is an energetic, upbeat, indefatigable personality who never runs out of energy—just as the battery runs longer than others.
- The Zara personality of being daring, trendy, exciting, spirited, and imaginative affects people's perceptions of Zara, its stores, and its products.
- Michelin's strong and dynamic personality, as reflected by the Michelin Man, implies that its tires will have strength and agility.
- Wells Fargo, as represented by the stagecoach, reflects an independent, cowboy type that delivers reliably. Although competitors may actually deliver superior reliability and safety of assets, because of the stagecoach, Wells wins the battle of perceptions.

Provide Energy

A strong brand personality such as that surrounding Mercedes, Porsche, or Jeep can provide energy by adding interest and involvement; it effectively amplifies brand perceptions and experience. Most hotel chains suffer from being undifferentiated and even bland. In contrast, the Joie de Vivre hotel chain created energy with personality-driven hotels around concepts like a neo-deco feel, the rock scene, literary salons of the 1930s, the theater setting, or French Chateau styling. All airlines seem very similar until you consider the energy created by the personality profiles of brands like Singapore, Southwest, and Virgin. Think of the energy surrounding the personality of the AXE brand—the brand as-a-person is obsessed by and successful with attractive women.

Define a Brand Relationship

A brand personality can define a relationship between people. A trustworthy, dependable, conservative personality might be boring, but nonetheless reflect characteristics valued in a financial advisor, a lawn service, or a physician. A personality of a competent leader will be a valued attribute of a CEO or manager. The concept of a relationship between a brand and a person, analogous to that between two people, provides a different perspective on how brand personality might work.[2] For example, consider the following relationship metaphors:

- An old-fashioned mother—down-to-earth, honest, genuine, reliable, and always-there-for-you such as Campbell's Soup or Pepto Bismol.
- A well-liked and respected family member—warm, sentimental, and family-oriented, linked to growing up such as Sun-Maid Raisins, Chevrolet, or a local bank.
- A person who you respect as a teacher, minister or business leader—accomplished, talented, and competent as represented by IBM, McKinsey, or the *Wall Street Journal*.
- A boss who exercises power or a rich relative—pretentious, wealthy, and condescending, perhaps reflecting for some the personality of the Master's Golf Tournament, Trump Towers, or Lexus (with gold trim).
- A stimulating companion—interesting with incredible stories such as those of the Dos Equis beer spokesperson who was labeled as the most interesting man who, among other things, speaks Spanish in Russian, bowls overhand, and has inside jokes with strangers.
- A companion for an outdoor adventure—athletic, rugged, and outdoorsy personality, such as REI or Eddie Bauer.
- A weekend fun companion—fun, energetic, and social. Pepsi might be better than Coke.

The last three personality descriptors all involve a type of friend relationship. A friend can also be bar buddies (Miller Lite), caring, or just comfortable to be around. Refining the relationship definition, whether it is a friend relationship or another, can help provide clarity and depth.

Guiding Brand-Building Programs

Tactically, the brand personality concept and vocabulary communicates to those who must implement the brand-building effort. Knowing that the brand aspires to be warm and approachable guides every brand association, including its product category, positioning, attributes, use experiences, user imagery, applications, firm values, and so on.

Communication programs, in particular, need guidance. As a practical matter, decisions need to be made about the communication package, including advertising, packaging, promotions, events, customer touchpoints, digital programs, and more. If the brand is specified only in terms of attribute associations, little guidance is provided. To say that TaylorMade golf equipment is of high quality with an innovative design does not give much direction. However, to say that TaylorMade-as-person is a demanding professional conveys much more. A brand personality statement provides depth and texture, making it more feasible to keep the communication effort on strategy.

Help Understand the Customer

The brand personality metaphor can also help a manager gain an in-depth understanding of consumer perceptions of the brand. Instead of asking about attribute perceptions, which can be boring and intrusive, asking people to describe a brand personality is often involving and can result in more accurate and richer insights into feelings and relationships. The arrogant and powerful personality ascribed to Microsoft, for example, provides a deeper understanding about the nature of the relationship between Microsoft and its customers. Or the personality construct might be a better entry into understanding the calmness emotion associated with Celestial Tea than a discussion of attributes.

Exploring what a brand-as-person might say to you can be a good way to uncover emotional response to brands. When this approach was applied to a credit card, one customer segment for which the brand-as-a-person was perceived as being dignified, sophisticated, educated, a world traveler, and confident believed that the card would make very positive supportive comments to them, such as:

"My job is to help you get accepted."
"You have good taste."

A second "intimidated" segment for which the credit card brand was perceived as being sophisticated and classy but snobbish, aloof, and condescending believed that the card-as-a-person would make negative comments, such as:

"I'm so well-known and established that I can do what I want."

"If I were going to dinner, I would not include you in the party."

The two user segments had remarkably similar perceptions of the brand, but the perceived attitude of the brand toward the customer was a big discriminator of the attitude toward the brand.

WHAT BRAND PERSONALITY?

Should brand personality be part of your brand vision? And if so, should it be a core vision element, an important driver of brand differentiation and the customer relationship, or an extended element? Brands like Virgin, Harley-Davidson, Nike, Tiffany, and MUJI have brand personality as a core element. If the brand personality is used to enrich the brand understanding or soften a negative image it would be an extended element. MetLife's "Peanuts characters" personality, for instance, would be an extended element.

Not all brands should aspire to have a personality, especially as a core vision element. They can and will compete on other dimensions. In fact, the brands that have a brand personality as a core brand vision are in the minority. The use of a brand personality as an extended brand vision element is, however, more common. In any case, the possibility of including a brand personality should be considered explicitly, as it is a good vehicle to make sure the brand vision is complete. In many cases, for example, brand strategists will forget that they could use some sources of brand energy. Asking the brand personality questions can bring such a need to the table.

The specification of what brand personality would help is a key step in the brand vision process. A helpful exercise is to ask customers and employees to describe the brand-as-a-person. The result can provide both insight and guidance. The final judgment about the nature of the desired brand personality will depend on what roles the brand personality will play. Will it be to represent and communicate attributes, to provide energy, to define a relationship, to guide decisions that affect the brand, or to have another defined purpose, such as to soften an association standing in the way of gaining loyalty?

The selection of a brand personality will then have to be implemented. If the implementation process is difficult or awkward, then the brand personality may have to be reviewed. If, however, there are ways to bring the brand personality to life through symbols, a charismatic CEO, an advertising campaign, a sponsorship, or a customer interaction style, then the brand personality may be a winner and may even play an expanded role.

One point of departure is a brand personality scale that was developed in a classic study. Respondents assessed the personality of sixty well-known brands using 114 personality traits. The study findings, that the personality assessments represented fifteen personality traits grouped into five personality factors, provided a base-line feel for the scope of personality dimensions and a starting point when generating an aspirational brand personality.[3] The traits were as follows:

- **Sincerity**—Home Depot, Hallmark, Chevrolet, Schwab
  - Down-to-Earth—Family-Oriented, Small-Town, Blue Collar, All-American
  - Honest—Ethical, Thoughtful, Caring
  - Genuine—Authentic, Ageless, Wholesome, Classic, Old-Fashioned
  - Friendly—Warm, Happy, Cheerful, Sentimental
- **Excitement**--Porsche, Absolut, Red Bull, Virgin
  - Exciting--Daring, Trendy, Off-Beat, Flashy, Provocative
  - Spirited--Adventurous, Lively, Outgoing, Young
  - Fun--Surprising, Imaginative, Unique, Humorous, Artistic
  - Innovative--Aggressive, Up-to-Date, Contemporary, Independent
- **Competence**—AMEX, CNN, IBM, Toyota
  - Trustworthy—Careful, Reliable, Hard-Working, Secure, Efficient
  - Serous—Intelligent, Technical, Competent
  - Successful—Leader, Confident, Influential
- **Sophistication**—Tiffany, Four Seasons, Mercedes, Calvin Klein
  - Upper-Class—Sophisticated, Glamorous, Good-Looking, Confident
  - Charming—Feminine, Smooth, Sexy, Gentle
- **Ruggedness**—Levi's, REI, Harley-Davidson, Jeep
  - Tough—Strong, Rugged
  - Outdoorsy—Masculine, Western, Active, Athletic

This set of fifteen traits provides one perspective, but can and should be augmented for nearly any context. For specific product markets some of these may not be relevant and others will emerge. That is especially true in different cultures. When the study was replicated in Japan and Spain, the Ruggedness dimension was not to be found. Instead, a Calmness dimension emerged. In Spain there was also a Passionate dimension.[4]

Like a person brand, an offering brand is not generally described by a single personality dimension. Harley-Davidson, for example, is a macho, America-loving, freedom-seeking person who is willing to break out from confining societal norms of dress and behavior. Patagonia is an environmental activist who is passionate about the outdoors as a participant and protector. Ben & Jerry's Ice Cream is about environmental activism, giving back to the community, and having fun doing nutty things. Some brands might even have conflicting dimensions, Microsoft, for example, might be perceived as arrogant well as competent. The challenge is to manage that conflict so that the "right" personality dominates perceptions and discussions.

MAKING IT HAPPEN

A personality needs to be created and supported. This effort can be based in part on a visible CEO, brand positioning, attributes, packaging, price, user imagery, sponsorships, the category involved, and much more. Sometimes a personality option will emerge from some brand association like a symbol or sponsorship. If a personality cannot be created with authenticity, then its viability as part of the brand and its image should be reviewed.

THE BOTTOM LINE

A brand personality can help communicate offering attributes, provide energy, define a customer relationship, guide brand-building programs, and shed insight into customer's attitudes and behavior. Selecting the right personality will depend on the brand image, its vision, and the role that personality will play going forward. Brands that are blessed with a personality have a big edge in terms of gaining and keeping visibility, differentiation, and loyalty, because it is usually difficult and ineffective to copy a personality.

Chapter 5

THE ORGANIZATION AND ITS HIGHER-PURPOSE DIFFERENTIATE

Purpose-driven companies have a huge *competitive advantage.*
Employees and customers are hungry for purpose.
—Rich Karlgaard, Publisher, *Forbes*

Just when you have an offering innovation that powers a meaningful differentiation, a competitor brand copies you. Or, worse, appears to copy.

What a competitor brand cannot copy is an organization—its people, culture, heritage programs, assets, and capabilities—because that is unique. Thus, any point of differentiation or basis of a customer relationship that is driven by the organization rather than by offering characteristics will be enduring and resistant to competitor brands.

The organization is usually represented and driven by its values. What is important to the organization? What is at its core? What is the priority in terms of strategy, performance measurement, and programs? Is there a focus on quality, innovation, social programs, customer service, or some other fundamental tenet? And why? What is it about its heritage, programs, strategy, or value proposition that make one or more values stand out?

Organizational values can be useful for any brand. However, in the case of service offerings, where the customer will have contact with people in the organization, organizational values will be particularly important. That can also be said about BtoB firms, where the expectation that the organization will have the necessary assets and skills to deliver behind the promise and the will to stand behind the offering can be a critical consideration.

The organizational brand can represent a firm, but it also can be an organizational unit within a firm, such as Ford's Lincoln, Disney's ESPN, or P&G's Tide. The challenge for these organizational units is to create and communicate their own values with supporting heritage, cultures, and programs.

HOW ORGANIZATIONAL VALUES WORK

The brand-as-an-organization perspective, summarized in Figure 3, potentially contributes to a customer relationship in three ways: to support a value proposition, to provide credibility as an endorser, and to create a higher purpose.

Supports a Value Proposition

Organizational values and associated programs can provide a "reason to believe" behind functional benefits that are the basis for a value proposition. An organization that has a reputation for delivering high-quality and innovative offerings, and has attracted people and developed programs that reflect that culture, supports a value proposition around quality and performance. A GE jet engine can be described in terms of specs and performance data. However, just the fact that it comes from GE can be a more persuasive argument that the product will deliver at a high level of performance. People believe the stated or implied assertion that Lexus delivers the highest quality because of the belief that the Lexus organization has quality as an organizational value.

An organizational reputation around a priority like quality or concern for customers is enduring. At any given time, there is always a competitor who can outspec you. Even when you are superior, there are always some segments that are uninformed or unconvinced. Having strength in an intangible dimension provides an advantage that is more durable in such a market. For example, many buy Samsung because of its reputation as an innovative technology firm, even when the product in question may not be the most advanced.

The value proposition of a new offering is often based on the claim that it contains a breakthrough advance that can too often sound like puffery. A perception of an innovative organization can help support such a claim. Kevin Keller of Dartmouth and I conducted an experiment to explore the impact of corporate image on customer acceptance of a new product outside the current range of a firm's products.[1] Four different corporate images—innovative, environmentally conscious, community minded, or neutral—were created in four settings—baked goods, personal care products, dairy products, and over-the-counter drugs. An innovative corporate image was found to be markedly more effective at making prospective new products be perceived as not only more innovative but of higher quality.

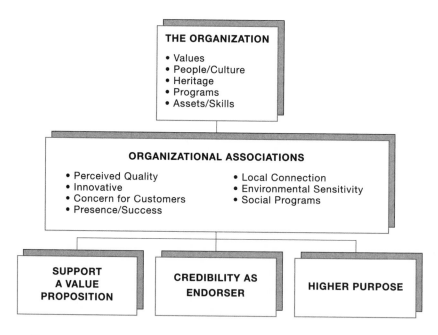

How Organizational Associations Provide Differentiation
Figure 3

Provides Credibility as Endorser

A brand representing an organization, even when it is acting as an endorser rather than an offering brand, can provide credibility. Kashi, Schwab, and Google, for example, can enhance the credibility of claims that an endorsed offering brand like GoLean, OneSource Select List, and Gmail is making. An endorser brand is especially important when a new and different offering is introduced under an unfamiliar brand name. It can make a big difference in a new product innovation program by reducing customer "risk."

The role of the endorser is to affirm that any endorsed offering brand will deliver on its promise. Marriott's Fairfield Inn is very different from a Marriott hotel, but the Marriott endorsement signals that Marriott will stand behind its endorsed brand. One basis of this assumption is that the organization is so competent, marshals so impressive a set of resources, and is so trustworthy that any endorsed brand will be capable of delivering. Another is that the endorser organization has its reputation at stake, and any offering inadequacy would affect that reputation and simply would not and could not be allowed to happen.

A Higher Purpose—A Basis for a Relationship

The higher purpose is an overriding organizational objective that is worth doing because it improves some people's lives. Crayola's higher purpose is to help parents and teachers raise inspired, creative children, certainly more ambitious and ennobling than selling crayons. The higher purpose of Tanita, the Japanese maker of personal and professional scales to measure weight and body fat, is to help people improve their health by better eating. The Tanita purpose was made visible by their well-known employee cafeteria featuring healthy meals, a cookbook used by some 10 percent of Japanese families, and, ultimately, by a successful restaurant, all based on a "better for you" menu.

The higher purpose provides the basis of a relationship with customers, raising the organization above the "my brand is better than your brand" competition and the noise that goes with it. In doing so, such a relationship can be stronger and more impervious to competition than a relationship based on functional benefits. It also can provide satisfaction and even inspiration to employees, as discussed in Chapter 14.

A customer can connect to an organization because of respect for and admiration of its higher purpose. People may admire the effort by the Dove brand to orient girls and women to real beauty and building self-esteem. Or Disney's effort to attack kid obesity. Or Apple's dream of creating insanely great products. Or the Discovery Channel's ability to help people explore. Those customers that are touched by a higher-purpose idea will want to support it and be part of the "family."

The higher purpose can lead to a "liking" relationship. MUJI, the Japanese retailer, is liked by its devotees who are attracted to its vision around simplicity, moderation, humility, self-restraint, serenity, and promoting the natural environment (MUJI has several wilderness parks). Products at MUJI are designed to be understated and functional, not glitzy—maximizing sales is not the criteria. Liking can be based on being stimulated or inspired. Asian Paints (the third largest paint firm in India) is liked by customers who are inspired by its effort to go beyond selling paint to giving people confidence in their ability to select colors for interior painting. Southwest Airlines has stimulated liking with its higher purpose of injecting humor and fun into air travel to reduce the stress and boredom.

Being liked influences the way some information, whether positive or negative, is screened and processed. And when "liking" is engendered, it tends to cling.

ORGANIZATIONAL VALUES

There are dozens of organizational values that can be used in any given context, but seven keep resurfacing as driving forces. Understanding them will also provide a more general look at the concept of how values work and, in particular, the role that the organizational culture and reward systems play into these values.

Perceived Quality

A basic organizational function is to create offerings that consistently deliver high quality with respect to their brand promise. Perceived quality is a key consideration in nearly every choice context. A distinction is made between the argument that an offering is of the highest quality, and the more general claim that the organization so values and rewards high quality that it will ensure that of all its offerings can be expected to live up to that standard. Thus, a customer does not have to analyze specifications, read reviews, and talk to other users. Just knowing what organization designed and delivered the offering is enough. The famous lines "Quality Is Job One" at Ford, "We try harder" at Avis, or "You're in good hands" from State Farm reflect an organization-wide commitment to quality. But of course those taglines need to be credibly backed up with programs and the right customer experience or they will ring hollow.

Innovation

Being innovative is one of the most universal organizational values. Most organizations want to be known as being innovative in order to be associated with advanced offerings, a dynamic company, and a contemporary brand with energy and movement. An innovative reputation is regarded as imperative for firms in which technology plays a role in the offerings, or when offering advances are part of the value proposition.

Concern for Customers

Many organizations, from Zappos.com to Lexus to the Mayo Clinic, have as a core value a drive to be customer oriented, to always place the customer first. They, and others so oriented, have created significant loyalty based on a visible culture and programs to please customers. If a firm can credibly communicate such a philosophy, customers not only gain confidence in the products and services, but also feel that someone cares for them. It is a lot easier to like someone who likes you.

Several corporate brands have made the concept of being a friend or colleague to customers as one of the defining and driving elements of their brand vision, The friend and colleague metaphor, as noted in Chapter 4, is very powerful because a relationship so defined implies that the brand will deliver what the customer wants with honesty, caring, dependability, and respect.

Success/Size

Success, size, and longevity suggest competence, substance, and even excellence. They breeds confidence, positive attitudes, and sometimes prestige (especially in Asia). People are reassured by an organization with the resources to back up its products and a reputation for having been in business for the long term, especially in high-tech markets. Just being known and visible can also affect the use experience and thus reinforce a reputation. Taste tests of packaged goods have been shown to be affected by whether the brand name is familiar.

A successful firm is perceived to be good at what they do. Customers are reassured knowing that other customers have selected the brand. For decades, GE created a strong brand mainly by the aura of marketplace success that was validated by a visible CEO and the stock market. Further, there is comfort behind the old, now somewhat anachronistic, expression "you can't get fired for buying IBM." A reputation for success can provide justification for a buy decision.

Going Local

One strategic option is to be perceived as a local brand from a local company. Thus, Lone Star, "The National Beer of Texas," is part of the community and draws upon the fact that a segment identifies with the Texas heritage of Lone Star, which goes back over a century. Buying and drinking Lone Star can thus be a way to express a pride and attachment to Texas.

The local route does not need to be restricted to a local firm, however. Some of the most successful brands in Europe are successful because they have chosen to adopt a local flavor; they are accepted as part of the local culture and are not viewed as being foreign. Thus, the U.S.-based Holiday Inn is considered "local" in many parts of Europe, particularly in Germany. The English consider Heinz to be their brand even though it is a U.S. brand with a German name. GM's Opel is considered German in Germany and Ford is thought of as a UK brand in that country.

Environmental Programs

It is amazing how many firms have signed on to environmental programs and have delivered substance as well as talk. They believe it is the right thing to do, it makes employees feel good about their firm, and it provides a way to connect to the substantial group of customers who care. The segment that will resonate with sustainability efforts may be a minority, maybe 10 to 40 percent of the market, depending on the context and the definition of "caring," but this group still can make the difference between market success and mediocrity.

Unilever is a good and not atypical example. In 2010 the firm launched the Unilever Sustainable Living Plan where they committed to a ten-year journey toward sustainable growth. The plan has three significant objectives:[2]

- Help more than a billion people to improve their health and well-being. During a seven year period more than 35 million people gained access to safe water due to Unilever's efforts.
- Halve the environmental footprint of its products by increasing the percent of Unilever's energy use that is renewable.
- Allow Unilever to source 100 percent of their agricultural raw materials sustainably. In the first two years of the plan, the percentage went from 14 percent to 24 percent.

Underpinning these three broad goals are more than fifty time-bound targets, from the sourcing of raw materials to the use of their products in the home.

Social Programs

A higher-purpose goal can also focus on addressing social needs with programs, especially those that have a fit with the organization and can employ organizational assets and skills. For example:

- McDonald's has the Ronald McDonald House, started nearly forty years ago, which provides housing for families whose children are hospitalized, and the Ronald McDonald Care Mobile, which provides health care for needy children.

- KitchenAid has Cook for the Cure, a program that has raised money since 2001 for the Susan G. Komen for the Cure (for breast cancer) organization.
- P&G's Live, Learn, and Thrive cause helps children in need around the world get off to a healthy start, receive access to education, and build skills for life.
- Toms gives away a pair of shoes to a child in need for every shoe sold. The tagline is "One for One."

MANAGING THE ORGANIZATIONAL BRAND

An organizational value needs to be supported not only with a strong culture and reward structure, but with a real commitment over time, with resources employed and outcomes measured. It can't just be verbal; there has to be real substance driven by a strong consistent belief that the values are right for the organization and its strategy. And there needs to be a culture and programs guided by a plan to make the values come alive.

But even significant substance will rarely lead to credit in the marketplace. As a result, one of the key benefits of having strong organizational values is lost. Getting credit in the market place can be challenging, because nearly all competitors claim the same set of values, and the values involved are often intangible, which makes their communication difficult. Some guidelines:

One approach is to create or leverage an offering that represents the value. In Japan, the top two brands with respect to being perceived as strong on social programs—out of a thousand brands tracked over ten years—were Toyota, where Prius told the story, and Panasonic, which had its energy-efficient appliances and energy-control systems to carry the flag.[3] In both cases the evidence was based on well-communicated products and thus was persuasive.

Another approach is to develop visible, branded, substantive programs that work and then support them relentlessly. Patagonia, for example, had a heritage of environmental concern, starting with their clean mountain climbing equipment in the 1970s, and has taken leadership roles in programs like the Conservation Alliance

(1989), where firms commit annual contributions used to fund conservation causes, and the Organic Exchange (2002), to promote organic cotton.

Patagonia's dramatic Common Threads initiative launched in 2005, aims to minimize the environmental cost of clothing through its programs to reduce, repair, reuse, and recycle clothing. *Reduce* means to forego buying articles of clothing unneeded in the first place. Patagonia actually ran a full page ad in the *New York Times* advising people not to buy one of their popular jackets because it took so much water and energy to make. *Repair* means to return clothing to Patagonia to have it repaired at nominal cost. *Reuse* means to donate a clothing item to charity, or sell it through eBay's Common Threads site or on the Patagonia website. *Recycle* means to return recyclable items to bins for that purpose; the raw material will be recycled into new Patagonia clothing.

The communication task is easier if it has an emotional component. PetSmart's Adopt-A-Pet program has saved the lives of more than five million pets, and each one has a story behind it. Unilever's effort to bring clean water to poverty-stricken areas in Bangladesh and elsewhere has global stories about the number of people aided, and individual stories about villages that had their lifestyles and health changed.

It helps if the programs are linked to the heritage of the organization. The heritage of a founder or event that established the essence of the brand can be an important driver of both communication and inspiration. A story of a brand's roots will tend to be rich and relevant, making the brand stand out from product brands. Chapter 14 provides such stories involving brands like L.L. Bean and Nordstrom.

THE BOTTOM LINE

Organizational values, such prioritizing quality, innovation, or customers, which generate brand differentiation and a basis for a customer relationship, are enduring because they are difficult to copy. They can represent and thus communicate a value proposition, provide credibility as an endorser, and create a higher purpose valued by customers and employees. One challenge is to identify what organizational values will work for a brand. Another is to find ways to get credit for them in the marketplace.

Chapter 6

GET BEYOND FUNCTIONAL BENEFITS

You cannot win the hearts of customers
unless you have a heart yourself.
—Charlotte Beers, J Walter Thompson

When identifying the top print advertisements and best headline in the last century of advertising, the one written in 1926 by a young copywriter named John Caples, only one year on the job, always comes up in the conversation. The ad is known by its head:

"They laughed when I sat down at the piano—but when I started to play."

His assignment? Entice people to buy piano lessons by correspondence from the U.S. School of Music.

Under a picture of a young man at a party sitting down to play the piano, the headline set the stage and indeed summarized the story, which was recounted in detail in the body of the ad. The hero was ridiculed by the guests when he sat down, but the ridicule turned to accolades and applause when he began to play, only a few months after starting the correspondence course. The ad was not only critically acclaimed but, more to the point, brought in a lot of customers.

There is a lot to learn today from this ad. There was almost nothing about the offering or the process of learning to play that surrounded it. Rather, the ad told a story in graphic detail about what happened to someone who took the correspondence course. Most remarkable, the ad shows that functional benefits are not the sweet spot of persuasion and communication. Rather, what grabs people are emotional, self-expressive, and social benefits. There is the emotion felt not only by the piano player who excelled in a pressure context, but by those hearing the story who are bursting with pride that he did it. There is the self-expressive benefit, the ability of the person to express his talent, his perseverance, and his ability to face down doubters and those who ridiculed. And there is the social benefit, when the man became not only accepted into a desirable reference group but an admired member.

All too common is what I call the product-attribute fixation trap, in which the strategic and tactical management of the brand is excessively focused on product attributes and functional benefits. Product attributes, such as the gas mileage of a Ford Fusion, the quality of Kraft products, the competence of BofA, or the fact that Subaru excels in snow are assumed dominant in the brand relationship.

A functional benefit focus is appealing. Our assumption, especially if we reside in the high tech or a BtoB sector, is that customers are rational and will be swayed by functional benefits. The assumption is based on instinct and the knowledge that customers when asked why they buy this brand or avoid that one give functional reasons because that is what comes to their mind and because anything else would not reflect well on them and their decision making. The resulting insights support the product-attribute-fixation trap and often have an inordinate influence on strategy.

This "rational person" view of customers is comfortable but usually wrong. Customers are almost always far from rational, as was documented by several writers, such as Dan Ariely in *Predictably Irrational*.[1] We see it every day. Research on trucks, for example, suggests that rational attributes like durability, safety features, options, and power are said by customers to be the most important. Yet more intangible attributes like "cool styling," being "fun to drive," and "feeling powerful" are more likely to influence decisions of customers who often cannot or will not admit that such frills are really important to them. There is little doubt that even airlines, buying aircraft with piles of detail, will in the end be influenced by their gut feel. In most contexts, customers lack the motivation, the time, the information, or the competence to make decisions to maximize performance outcomes and will project functional benefits from other brand associations.

Even worse, strategies based on functional benefits are often strategically ineffective. Customers may not believe the benefit represents a compelling reason to buy the brand. Or they may assume that all brands are adequate with respect to a functional benefit. In the hotel business, for example, check-out efficiency is important, but all hotels may be perceived to be about the same on that dimension. Most discouraging of all, competitors may copy or appear to copy any functional advantage.

Functional benefit strategies are also limiting because they often confine the brand, especially when it comes to responding to changing markets or exploring brand extensions. The fact that Heinz means slow-pouring, rich catsup may limit its role in extension strategies, whereas the association of Contadina with Italians provides more extension flexibility. A source of attribute strength may, in fact, become a liability.

Thus, it makes sense to move beyond functional benefits and the offering. The use of organizational associations (innovation, a drive for quality, and concern for the environment, for example) and brand personality (like being perceived to be upscale, competent, and trustworthy), covered in the last two chapters, do just that. Another approach is to consider emotional, self-expressive, and social benefits as part of the brand vision and as a basis for the value proposition.

EMOTIONAL BENEFITS

An emotional benefit relates to the ability of the brand to make the buyer or user feel something during the purchase process or use experience. "When I buy or use this brand I feel_____." Thus, a customer can feel excited while driving a Porsche, relaxed when having a tea from Celestial Seasonings, in control when using TurboTax, rugged when wearing Levi's, or warm when receiving a Hallmark card. Evian, with its "Another day, another chance to feel healthy." associated itself with the satisfied feeling that comes from a work out. Cars.com, with its side-by-side comparison tool, replaces drama and stress in the car-buying experience with a feeling of calm and confidence.

Emotional benefits add richness and depth to the brand and the experience of owning and using the brand. Without the memories that Sun-Maid raisins evokes, the brand would border on commodity status. The familiar red package links many users to the happy days of helping mom in the kitchen (or the idealized childhood for those who wished that they had such experiences). The result can be a different use experience, one with feelings, and a stronger brand.

The strongest brand identities have both functional and emotional benefits. A study by Stuart Agres supports this assertion.[2] A laboratory experiment involving shampoo showed that the addition of emotional benefits (you will look and feel terrific) to functional benefits (your hair will be thick and full of body) enhanced the appeal. A follow-up study found that 47 TV commercials that included an emotional benefit had a substantially higher effectiveness score (using a standardized commercial laboratory testing procedure) than 121 commercials that had only a functional benefit.

SELF-EXPRESSIVE BENEFITS

People express their own or an idealized self in a variety of ways such as job choice, friends, attitudes, opinions, activities, and lifestyles. Brands that people like, admire, discuss, buy, and use also provide a vehicle for expressing either an actual or ideal self-image. "When I buy or use this brand I am_____." Delivering self-expressive benefits is the essence of being a charismatic brand.

A brand does not have to be Harley to deliver self-expressive benefits. A person can be cool by buying clothes at Zara, successful by driving a Lexus, creative by using Apple, a nurturing mother by preparing Quaker Oats hot cereal, smart by attending Yale, avant garde by owning a picture from a trendy artist, frugal and unpretentious by shopping at Kmart, or adventurous and active by owning REI camping equipment. Using a Schwab account is a signal that a person can manage an investment portfolio. Their tagline—"Own your tomorrow"—expresses that expression of independence.

Each person has multiple roles. A woman may be a wife, lawyer, mother, tennis player, music buff, and hiker. For each role, a person will have an associated self-concept, a need to express that self-concept, and a set of brands that help satisfy that need.

When a brand provides a self-expressive benefit, the connection between the brand and the customer is likely to be heightened. Consider the difference between using Oil of Olay (which has been shown to heighten one's self-concept of being gentle and mature, but also exotic and mysterious) and Jergens or Vaseline Intensive Care Lotion, neither of which provides a comparable self-expression benefit.

SOCIAL BENEFITS

A brand can enable a person to be part of a social group and thereby convey social benefits. "When I buy or use this brand, the type of people I relate to are _____." A social benefit is powerful because it provides a sense of identity and belonging—very basic human drives. Most people need to have a social niche, whether it is a family, a work team, a recreation group, etc. This social point of reference can play a role in defining a person and influencing what brands he or she buys, uses, and values.

Hyatt restructured and rebranded its extended-stay hotels around a social benefit position. The Hyatt House brand focused on enabling a social feel and experience. Added was a large lounge, a fire pit and barbecue grill on the patio, an advanced entertainment system, a pool table, and a multiuse island in its suites, all designed to optimize "getting together." Further, the breakfast and cocktail hour experience was enhanced to create more social opportunities.

When a brand-driven community is formed around a person's lifestyle and values, a social benefit is created. Kraft Kitchens formed a community around cooking dishes and meals that are tasty, healthy, and easy to prepare. The community provides a sense of belonging to a group that shares an interest and accepts them as members. The more engaged a person is, the more intense will be the feeling of belonging. The power of communities is explored in Chapters 11 and 12.

Another type of social benefit occurs when a brand defines or links to a reference group, a group in which an individual identifies and values. An individual may not be part of a reference group, or at least an active part, but so identifies with it that it becomes important in his or her life. Drinkers of Opus One wine may have an affinity to a reference group of Opus One connoisseurs that provides both identity and belonging, even if they don't know any personally. Starbuck's users might in effect be saying: "When I go to Starbucks I am part of a closed club of coffee and coffee house aficionados, even if I don't interact with any." The reference group can be aspirational. "When playing with a Titleist Pro V1 golf ball, I am among a group of really good golfers."

COMBINING BENEFITS

These three benefits are often related, and a brand or its associated programs can actively involve two or all three benefits. BeautyTalk, the Sephora web-based community around beauty, for example, could provide a satisfying emotional benefit from looking good, a self-expressive benefit of being knowledgeable about, if not an expert in, an area of importance, in addition to the social benefit of being part of a community. Zipcar provides the emotional benefit surrounding the cool experience of activating a conveniently located car with a Zipcard, the self-expressive benefit of avoiding the cost and hassle of car ownership, and the social benefit of being part of an urban, energy conserving group. That was also the case in the ad "They laughed...." discussed at the outset.

When multiple benefits are present, it can be useful to prioritize them, because it can matter which perspective dominates. It can impact the way that the benefits are enhanced and brought to light. For example, emotional benefits tend to involve the act of using the product (wearing a cooking apron confirms oneself as a gourmet cook), whereas self-expressive benefits tend to focus on the consequence of using the product (feeling proud and satisfied because of the appearance of a well-appointed meal), and social benefits would picture others affected by the use experience (the feelings of others participating in cooking or attending the meal). These differences suggest that it will be helpful to know which perspective is being used.

WHICH BENEFITS?

How can potential emotional, self-expressive, or social benefits be identified? One approach is to look at the experience of the most loyal customers. In all likelihood, they have experiences that go beyond functional benefits. The potential to expand their experiences to a larger group of customers can then be explored.

Another approach is to think of benefits that the offering and brand could potentially create if the offering were expanded or if the right programs were initiated. In making these analyses, employing research techniques that focus on basic motivations, creative thinking, and exploring how other brands have gone beyond functional benefits will be helpful.

Still another route is to consider having a strong personality or dialing up the organizational values. Both of these paths tend to provide emotional, self-expressive, or social benefits.

THE BOTTOM LINE

Brand personality, organizational associations, emotional benefits, self-expressive benefits, and social benefits are powerful drivers of brand relationships and loyalty, making them both broader and deeper than functional benefits defined by the offering. They go to very basic needs and motivations. The ability of competitors to disrupt the relationship based on a functional benefit appeal becomes lessened. There is a lot of upside to getting beyond functional benefits.

Chapter 7

CREATE "MUST HAVES" RENDERING COMPETITORS IRRELEVANT

You don't want to be considered just the best of the best; you want to be considered the only one who does what you do.
—**Jerry Garcia, The Grateful Dead**

The brand home run is when the point of differentiation becomes a "must have" that defines a new subcategory (or sometimes a new category) and renders competitors irrelevant. A substantial group of customers will not consider any brand lacking the "must have."[1]

Such an innovation will not happen frequently, but when it does, brand strategists need to seize that opportunity, recognizing that something bigger than a point of differentiation is present, and manage it accordingly. The firm needs to not only develop a "must have," but also bring it to market and then build barriers to competitors, so the luxury of competing in a market for which its brand has a monopoly or near-monopoly will not be short-lived. It is not easy, but the upside is enormous.

A "must have" can be based on a transformational innovation that creates an offering with characteristics that customers must have. It changes what is bought and used. Transformational innovation is a game changer. Take SalesForce.com championing cloud computing, Cirque du Soleil reinventing the circus, and Keurig creating the cup-at-a-time pod-style brewing system. It each case the innovation changes what is bought and used.

A "must have" can also come from substantial innovation, which will not change the basic characteristics of the offering but will significantly enhance it. A new "must have" feature or service will be added or one of the offering characteristics will be improved so dramatically that customers will now reject any option without it. Under Armour created a $1 billion clothing business based on new fabrics that absorb moisture and have superior breathability. The branded ingredient Kevlar provided a substantial innovative improvement, defining a subcategory in the body armor market.

An incremental innovation, one that will improve or strengthen brand preference with a "like to have" in the context of the existing subcategories (or categories), would not qualify.

The "must have" can improve or enhance the offering with:

- A **feature,** such as the high fiber content in Fiber One.
- A **benefit,** such as that provided by Nike Plus, the running shoe with a built-in chip that allows users to track and share their training data.
- An **appealing design,** such as those found in Apple products.
- A **system offering,** that combines components such as Siebel's CMR offering, which integrates suites of customer contact programs.
- A **new technology,** like IBM's supercomputer Watson.
- A **product** designed for a segment, such as Luna, the energy bar for women.
- A dramatically **low price point,** like that provided by JetBlue airlines.

A "must have" can also involve a basis for a customer relationship that does not involve the offering but is important to the customer, such as:

- A **shared interest,** such as Pampers Village, a go-to site for baby care.

- A **personality** that connects, such as the energy of Red Bull, the competence of Charles Schwab, the irreverence of Virgin, the humor of Southwest, or the exotic service of Singapore Airlines.
- A **passion,** such as that shown by Whole Foods Market for healthy, organic foods.
- **Organizational values,** such as being customer centered (Nordstrom), innovative (3M), global (Citibank), involved in social issues (Avon), or concerned about the environment (Patagonia).

In any case the "must have" is a characteristic or element of the brand relationship that is regarded by a segment of meaningful size as necessary for a brand to be considered and thus relevant.

THE "MUST HAVE" PAY OFF

Creating "must haves" through substantial or transformational innovation, making competitors irrelevant or less relevant, is not only desirable but is, with rare exceptions, the only way to grow. That bears repeating. With few exceptions, it is the only way to grow!

By far the more common strategy is to engage in what I call brand-preference competition, which focuses on making a brand preferred among the choices considered by customers in a defined subcategory. The goal is to beat competition through the use of incremental innovation to make the brand ever more attractive or less costly. "Faster, cheaper, better" is the mantra. Resources are expended on communicating more effectively with more clever advertising, more impactful promotions, more visible sponsorships, and more involving social media programs. You win by making your brand preferred as opposed to making your brand the only relevant brand, the only brand considered.

The problem is, "my brand is better than your brand" marketing rarely changes the marketplace, no matter how much marketing budget is available or how clever the incremental innovation. The stability of brand positions in nearly all markets is simply astonishing. There is just too much customer and market momentum. Brand-preference competition is also just "so not fun."

With few exceptions, the only time a market structure experiences any meaningful change is when a new "must have" is introduced with a major innovation. For example, the market-share trajectory within the Japanese beer industry changed only four times over four decades. In three of those occasions a brand created or got traction for a "must have" that defined a new subcategory (Asahi Dry Beer in 1986, Kirin Ichiban in 1990, and Kirin's Happoshu brand in the late 1990s).[2] The fourth was when two of the major subcategories, not just brands, were repositioned (in 1995 Asahi repositioned the dry subcategory and Kirin repositioned lager). All the marketing in other years simply did not move the needle.

You can look at any category and the result is the same. Only when new "must haves" are introduced, with rare exceptions, does the brand achieve real growth. In automobiles, for example, market dynamics were driven by innovations represented by brands such as Ford's Mustang and Taurus, the VW Bug, Mazda's Miata, Chrysler's Minivans, Toyota's Prius and Lexus, and BMW's MINI Cooper. In computers, the market was altered by new subcategories defined by DEC's minicomputer, Silicon Graphic's workstations, Sun's network servers, Dell's build-to-order PCs, and Apple's interface. In services, there is IDEO, the innovation firm, and Zipcar, the car-sharing service. In packaged goods, there is Odwalla, So-Be, and Dreyer's Slow Churned Ice Cream. In retailing, there is Whole Foods Markets, Zara, Best Buy's Geek Squad, IKEA, Zappos.com, and MUJI, the no-brand store. All introduced new "must haves" into the marketplace and achieved significant growth facing established competitors.

Creating a marketplace with weak or nonexistent competition has a huge potential payoff. It is Econ 101, the ticket to real growth in sales and profits. Consider the Chrysler minivan introduced in 1982 as the Plymouth Voyager and Dodge Caravan, which sold 200,000 vehicles during its first year, over 13 million since, and enjoyed sixteen years with no viable competitors. It literally carried Chrysler for nearly two decades. Enterprise-Rent-A-Car, the firm renting cars to people whose car was being repaired, enjoyed an even longer period with no real competition when all the other car rental companies went after business or vacationing travelers.

Many financial studies support the fact that creating new categories or subcategories pays off. For example, one study examined strategic moves by 108 companies. The 14 percent that were categorized as creating new categories had 38 percent of the revenues and 61 percent of the profits.[3] Another study analyzed the hundred fastest-growing U.S.

companies from 2009 to 2011 and found that the thirteen companies that were instrumental in creating their categories account for 53 percent of the incremental revenue growth and 74 percent of the incremental market capitalization growth over those three years.[4]

EVALUATING POTENTIAL "MUST HAVES"

Ideas for "must haves" can come from a host of perspectives such as unmet customer needs, unintended applications, under-served segments, market trends, channel dynamics, role models in other industries or countries, or new technologies. Organizations need to not only search for but, more importantly, recognize potential "must haves" and allow them to move forward. A crucial step is to evaluate the ideas so that only the best are resourced. That involves two judgments.

Is the Concept Significant to the Marketplace? Is There a "Must Have?"

Does the new concept represent a substantial or transformational innovation or an incremental one? One error, which can be termed the rosy picture bias, is to assume that a substantial innovation exists when in fact the market regards it as incremental. Innovation champions tend to inflate the prospects of a new concept because they become psychologically committed, and because, the concept's success might be pivotal in a career path while a failure will represent a professional setback. There is also organizational momentum—an offering that has been funded and become part of the plan is sometimes hard to terminate. So there needs to be a hard-headed, research-based judgment made on the market response to the innovation.

Another, often more serious, mistake is the "gloomy picture bias" leading to an erroneous judgment that an innovation will not succeed when it represents an opportunity to own a major new category or subcategory. The judgment could rely on market size estimates based on existing flawed products. Second, the wrong application or market might be targeted and the potential thus missed. Joint Juice, a product designed to reduce joint pain by making glucosamine in liquid form, found life when it went after an older demographic instead of young to middle-aged athletes. Third, there could be a flawed assumption that a niche market could not be scaled and the resulting market is too small. For that reason Coca-Cola avoided the water market for decades, a decision that, in retrospect, was a strategic disaster. Fourth, a technical problem may look more formidable that it is. Finally, estimates can be colored by the fact that people and organizations tend to be risk adverse because the cost of failure is only too evident.

Can the Offering Be Created?

Is the concept even feasible, especially if a technological breakthrough is needed? And even if the offering is feasible, does the organization have, or can it create, the needed people, systems, culture, and assets that may be required? And does the organization have the will to commit to the idea even with barriers and difficulties? There will be times in which the risks seem great, the rewards appear uncertain, alternative uses of the resources are appealing, and internal political support is weak. Without real organizational commitment, the new innovation may become underfunded and potentially doomed.

Is the timing right? Being first into the market is not necessary or even always desirable. In fact, the pioneering brand is often premature because the market, the technology, or the firm is not ready. Apple was not the pioneer for the iPod (Sony beat Apple by two years), the iPhone (the technology was up and running in Europe years before), or the iPad (Bill Gates of Microsoft introduced the Tablet PC some ten years earlier) but, in each case, Apple had the timing right. The technology was in place or around the corner, the firm had the assets and experience, and the value proposition had been market-tested, albeit with inferior technology. For all the talents of Steve Jobs, his genius at timing has gone underappreciated.

BUILD BARRIERS TO COMPETITION

Creating a "must have" that defines a new subcategory for which the relevance of competitors is weak or nonexistent will not be worthwhile unless barriers can be created to inhibit or prevent competitors from becoming relevant.

The ultimate barrier is **proprietary technology or expertise** that is protected by patents, copyrights, trade secrets, or intellectual capital not easily accessed or duplicated. Toyota has the Hybrid Synergy Drive developed for Prius that cannot be duplicated. Dreyer's Slow Churned Ice Cream is an offering based on technology that yields creamy, good-tasting ice cream that is low fat. Technology can also be protected by branding as described in Chapter 8.

Becoming a **moving target,** as Apple did by following the iPod with products like the nano, shuffle, iTouch, and iPad, and Gillette did with razors, from the Trac II to the Fusion ProGlide, makes the task of becoming relevant for competing brands difficult. Chrysler went for sixteen years without a serious competitor in the minivan category it created in part because they never let even two years pass without an innovation that upped the bar for competitors. In some cases, the innovation was substantial and created a new "must have." We saw, for example, sliding driver-side doors, removable back seats for storage, swivel seats, four-wheel drive, child-safety locks, and Easy-Out Roller Seats.

Moving beyond functional benefits can create significant barriers. While functional benefits are often quickly copied, it is much harder to copy self-expressive, social and emotional benefits, the values and culture of the organization, or the personality of the brand.

Brand equity, as represented by visibility, associations, and brand loyalty, provides a significant barrier. During the early phases of a new innovative offering there is the opportunity to use the "news" value of the innovation to enable visibility and communication efforts to build a strong brand. There is also the possibility for a brand to capture the customers most likely to value the "must haves" and keep them involved and happy. In that case, competitors will be faced with less appealing segments on which to build a business.

Be prepared to scale the concept. Scaling, creating, and controlling a broad customer base is also critical because as long as the offering is occupying a local market or limited distribution, there are unexposed potential customers that competitors can access. Further, it is simple math: spreading fixed costs like warehousing, back-office support, management, advertising, or brand development over a large sales base will result in a lower per-unit cost. Scaling can be resourced by bringing in partners. Häagen Dazs, for example, partnered with Dreyer's to get access to their distribution. But sometimes it means accepting the risk of overinvestment at the front end. A key to the success of the Chrysler minivan was a willingness to invest in capacity even though the firm was in a cash crisis.

The **authentic label** can be important barrier. The authentic brand is perceived to be real vs. phony, an innovator, a leader rather than a copier, reliable, and trustworthy. A brand does not have to be first to be the authentic brand, but it does need to be the first to get the concept right and to gain traction. Efforts to explain and build the category or subcategory will enhance a reputation for authenticity.

Flawlessly execution also generates a barrier to competitors, especially if it is based not only on what is done but on the values and organization behind it. That was certainly the case with Zappos.com. Zappos.com, with its ten values (including the "Wow!" experience and being a bit weird), provided the basis for hiring and the decision to have a 24/7 call center that would find a pizza for a customer if asked. The "being weird" value provided a way to add creative initiative into the staff and also created an esprit de corp. The resulting customer experience presented a high bar and would be hard to duplicate because it is based on the people, processes, and culture. It is easy to see what a firm is doing but hard to duplicate who they are.

Branded differentiators and becoming a **subcategory exemplar** are important barriers considered in the next two chapters.

THE BOTTOM LINE

Creating "must haves" that render competitors less relevant, and then building barriers to prevent them from becoming relevant is, with rare exceptions, the only way to grow and has been shown to lead to high profit pay-offs. A potential "must have" should be considered as a "must have" by the marketplace and should represent an offering the firm can deliver. A key component in "must have" initiatives is to create and manage barriers to prevent competitors from becoming relevant. A big subcategory-defining innovation with the potential to get traction in the marketplace does not happen often, but when it does, the opportunity should not be lost by being too risk adverse.

Chapter 8

TO OWN AN INNOVATION, BRAND IT

First they ignore you. Then they ridicule you.
Then they fight you. Then you win.
—Mahatma Gandhi

D ifferentiation is the key to winning with new offerings *and* old. There needs to be a point of difference that provides a reason to buy and to be loyal. The ultimate route to differentiation is to innovate—if not the offering itself then programs supporting or relating to the offering—creating a "must have."

What is not understood is the role of branding in turning innovations into marketplace difference-makers. If the innovation has the potential of making a substantial and ongoing point of differentiation (and this is a big "if"), it needs to be branded. Brand it or lose it!!! Otherwise it is difficult to communicate and way too easy to copy or to appear to copy.

By branding an innovation we create a "branded differentiator"; a branded and actively managed feature, ingredient, technology, service, or program that creates a meaningful, impactful point of differentiation for a branded offering over an extended time period.

69

For example, in 1999 the Westin hotel chain created the "Heavenly Bed," a custom-designed mattress set (by Simmons) with nine hundred coils, three versions of a cozy down blanket for three climates, a comforter with a crisp duvet, three high-quality sheets, and five goose-down pillows. This branded feature became a branded differentiator that really defined a new subcategory—hotels with premium beds—in a crowded category in which differentiation is a challenge.

A branded differentiator does not occur simply by slapping a name on an innovation. The definition suggests that there are rather demanding criteria that need to be satisfied. In particular, a branded differentiator needs to be meaningful in that it matters to customers, and impactful in that it is not a trivial difference. The Heavenly Bed was meaningful in that it addressed the heart of a hotel room—to provide a good night's sleep. It was also impactful. During the first year of its life, hotel sites that featured The Heavenly Bed had a 5 percent increase in customer satisfaction, a noticeable increase in perceptions of cleanliness, room decor, and maintenance, as well as significantly increased occupancy.

A branded differentiator also needs to warrant active management over time and justify brand-building efforts. The Heavenly Bed has received that treatment with an active set of brand-building programs. It was made available for purchase first through Westin and later at Nordstrom and elsewhere. Westin encouraged the buzz created by the novelty of a customer buying a hotel's bed. The concept was extended to The Heavenly Bath, which has custom-designed showers with dual shower heads, shower components, and accessories. The Westin Home Collection website became a place to order the bed, bedding, bath accessories, robes, and more.

A branded differentiator needs to be linked to the branded offering; it has a product-defining role. A challenge for Westin has been to generate a link to The Heavenly Bed to avoid having a customer fail to recall which hotel has this feature, or worse, attributing it to another chain. Having a prominent, exclusive Westin endorsement helps.

TYPES OF BRANDED DIFFERENTIATORS

A branded differentiator, as suggested by the definition, can best be described as either being a feature, ingredient, technology, service, or program affecting the offering.

A Branded Feature

A branded feature will represent a unique benefit. It can provide a graphic way to signal superior performance, and a vehicle to own that point of superiority over time. To accomplish this mission, it must be something of value to customers, truly differentiating, and linked to the branded offering.

Amazon has the 1-Click ordering feature that provides a familiar added value. Some Under Armour clothing contains ArmourBlock, which provides resistance to odor formation so that clothes stay fresher longer. Oral-B, "the brand more dentists use," provides value with its toothbrush with an "Indicator" that changes color when the brush needs changing, the Pro-Flex that bends to adjust to the contour of the teeth, and the wireless "Smartguide" of the Oral-B power brush. All of these branded features provide a clear augmentation of the brand's value proposition.

A branded feature can be based on an established brand. For example, Delta Airlines tried to own air traveler's "superior sleeping" experiences, by leveraging the Heavenly brand with its "Westin Heavenly" comforter and pillow. In that case, the challenge was not to explain the innovation but to connect it to Delta Airlines.

A Branded Ingredient

Another perspective is to brand an ingredient. Even if customers do not understand how the ingredient works, the fact that it was branded lends credibility to the explicit or implied claims. Recall Intel Inside? Few really knew what Intel had inside the computer, but they were still willing to pay 10 percent more just for the peace of mind that they were getting something reliable and advanced. Even though the customer might not realize how the ingredient adds value, in the long run there does need to be substance behind it, because the truth of a vacuous claim will eventually be exposed.

A branded ingredient can also be imported, thereby leveraging a brand with an established meaning, following, and visibility. Customers immediately know what they are being offered. Sony offers the Cyber-shot Digital Camera with Carl Zeiss Sonnar T Lens, using the Carl Zeiss brand to reassure buyers that the key component is the highest quality. An ice cream brand can add ingredients such as M&Ms or Snickers to provide a unique product that will not have to be explained to users well aware of the candy brands.

A Branded Technology

A technology breakthrough, if branded, can make a difference by providing a rationale and thus credibility for a value proposition. Dreyer's Slow Churned Ice Cream is based on a technology that provides creamy ice cream with low fat. Prius dominated the hybrid category for more than a decade, in part because of Toyota's Hybrid Synergy Drive, a technology that provides several benefits. GE HealthCare has SenoBright* contrast-enhanced spectral mammography, which helps resolve inconclusive diagnoses by highlighting areas of unusual blood flow patterns.

The branded technology provides power just because it is branded. But it also can provide a window into the substance behind the claim and help communicate it by providing a point of reference. The brands "Slow Churned Ice Cream," "Hybrid Synergy Drive," and "SenoBright*" are not only evocative, but provide a construct that can represent a complex topic. Without these brands the communication effort would become bulky, difficult, and perhaps infeasible.

A Branded Service

The classic way to differentiate a brand is to augment the offering with a branded service that then has the potential to be a branded differentiator. The Geek Squad, which provides installation and service for computer and entertainment systems, has repositioned Best Buy and its category. Schwab's Mutual Fund OneSource Select provides a screened list of options that helps investors sort out a confusing area. Google AdWords is a service for Google advertisers that has helped it develop a leadership position. General Motors pioneered the OnStar system, which provides automatic activation of air bag deployment to roadside assistance agencies, stolen vehicle location, emergency services, remote door unlock, remote diagnostics, and even concierge serves. Amazon's Kindle delivers books via the Whispernet.

The Apple store's amazing success has many drivers. One is its branded service, The Genius Bar, which addresses a real need and creates a person-to-person relationship that can diffuse problems and build fans. The Genius Bar was not an initial success, but Apple's commitment to the concept paid off with ownership of a "must have" point of distinction.

Branded Programs

Branded programs that broaden or supplement the offering can be the basis for differentiation. Kaiser Permanente has a host of programs under umbrella brands such as Live Healthy (information about improving health), Healthy Lifestyle Programs (active programs to promote healthy living), and My Health Manager. Dell has Idea Storm and Direct2Dell, by which customers can make suggestions and dialogue about issues. Hilton Honors is a key asset of Hilton.

A branded program can be separate from, or adjacent to, the actual offering. Harley-Davidson is more than a brand—it is an experience and a community supported by several branded programs that are not part of an effort to describe or sell motorcycles. The Harley-Davidson Ride Planner, for example, allows a person to create a ride plan given starting and ending points plus desired stops. The output is a detailed map that you can save and share with friends.

THE VALUE OF BRANDING IT

A valued feature, ingredient, technology, service, or program will serve to differentiate a product whether or not it is branded. Why brand it? There are several reasons, most of which go back to the basic value of a brand in any context. Basically, a brand introduces the potential to own the innovation, adds credibility, and helps the communication task.

First and foremost, a brand provides the potential to own an innovation because a brand is a unique indicator of the source of the offering. A successful innovation, in most contexts, will be copied or appear to be copied by other firms and the resulting point of differentiation can be short lived. But competitors cannot copy a brand that is owned.

With the proper investment in, and active management of, both the innovation and its brand, this ownership potential can be extended into the future indefinitely. A competitor may be able to replicate the feature, ingredient, technology, service, or program, but if it is branded, they will need to overcome the power of the brand. Another hybrid automobile brand can make claims about their power train, but there will only be one authentic Hybrid Synergy Drive, the one owned by Toyota. If the association between the branded feature (Hybrid Synergy Drive) and brand (Toyota) is strong enough, the Toyota brand could get credit for hybrid engine technology innovations by others.

Second, a brand can add credibility and legitimacy to a claim. The branded differentiator specifically says that the benefit was worth branding, and that an organization was willing to commit to expending resources to create and communicate a brand. The observer will instinctively believe that there must be a reason why it was branded. Imagine if Chevron attempted to explain why "Chevron gasoline" was different without the use of the Techron brand. It would not be persuasive or even feasible. Customers may not know how Techron works, but they do know that it was meaningful enough to be branded.

The ability of a brand to add credibility was rather dramatically shown in a remarkable study of branded attributes. Carpenter, Glazer, and Nakamoto, three prominent academic researchers, found that the inclusion of a branded attribute (such as "Alpine Class" fill for a down jacket, "Authentic Milanese" for pasta, and "Studio Designed" for compact disc players) justified a higher price in the eyes of the respondents.[1] Remarkably, the effect occurred even when the respondents were given information implying that the attribute was not relevant to their choice.

Third, a brand makes communication more efficient, feasible, and memorable. Customers may have a hard time recognizing the value of an innovation, especially if it is somewhat complex in face of the confusion and clutter created by competitors and the marketplace. The act of giving the innovation a name can help by providing a vehicle to summarize a lot of information. It is not necessary to know the details of a hospital's "Heart Club" or the "Pamper's Parenting Institute" because the brands can represent complex, detailed information that would be difficult to recall, but just knowing the brand and its general mission is usually enough. The job of linking the point of differentiation to the parent brand is also made much easier by a branded differentiator.

THE YIN AND YANG OF BRANDS

Warning!! The concept of a branded differentiator is not a license or excuse to brand all innovations. That is a recipe for over branding. An innovation needs to be a substantial advance or evolve a game-changer as seen in the eyes of a customer, not from a vested innovation champion. It also needs to merit investment over time because of its potential to create and hold a market advantage. That is much more likely to be the case if it can support ongoing innovation so that it can evolve, being a moving target for competitors. A brand is a long-term asset and requires active and ongoing management. If the opportunity will not support such an investment, branding it can be a big mistake.

An organization needs to develop a process that qualifies innovations and insures that only those that merit being branded are rewarded with a brand and the resources to build and leverage it over time. But when a powerful branded differentiator opportunity does emerge, it is important to seize the opportunity and use it to create and maintain a leadership position.

THE BOTTOM LINE

A branded differentiator is a branded and actively managed branded feature, ingredient, technology, service, or program that creates a meaningful, impactful point of differentiation for a branded offering over an extended time period. It provides a way to own an innovation, provide credibility to it, and make communication easier and more memorable. When it is warranted, and that can be a question mark, it can be a powerful part of the brand portfolio.

Chapter 9

FROM POSITIONING THE BRAND TO FRAMING THE SUBCATEGORY

Frames are mental structures that shape the way we see the world. If a strongly held frame doesn't fit the facts, the facts will be ignored and the frame will be kept.
—**George Lakoff,** UC Berkeley Professor of Linguistics

Positioning your brand represents short-term communication objectives. What is it you want to say to communicate, enhance, or reinforce your current brand promise? It should be based on those parts of the brand vision that will resonate with the market, support the current business strategy, and reflect the current reality of what the brand can credibly deliver. To be successful, it needs to involve an effective driving idea and set of programs that are integrated throughout the organization.

The brand position is about your brand and how it differs from, and is better than, other brands. Apple is differentiated in part around design, Dove provides moisturizing, and Whole Foods Markets believes in and understands organic food. It assumes a fixed category or subcategory and set of competitors.

Framing has a bigger agenda. It aims to change the way people perceive, discuss, and feel about the subcategory (or category) and as such can change what people are buying and which brands are relevant to that purchase. It represents *a very different perspective* on competing and winning. Instead of assuming that the subcategory definition and set of competitors are fixed, framing allows the scope and defining characteristics of the subcategory to be in play. The subcategory can be defined to reduce relevance of some brands and/or increase relevance of others.

One subcategory framing objective can be to make competitors less relevant, or even *irrelevant*. As described in Chapter 8, a defining characteristic can be put forward as a "must have" which competitors lack or show weakness. A brand is selected not because it is preferred over competitors, but because the defined subcategory is preferred and it is the most relevant (or only relevant) brand in the subcategory.

So Apple defines a subcategory of computers with superior design, Dove a subcategory of products that deliver moisturizing, and Whole Foods Markets a subcategory of food retailers that have a focus on organic food. Framing the subcategory changes the competitive task from "my brand is better than your brand" to "this is the subcategory you need to buy" and "my brand is relevant to that subcategory." The choice of the subcategory to buy is the first stage of the buying process and dominating this first stage can influence, if not dictate, which brands wins.

An alternative framing objective could be to broaden an existing attractive subcategory to include your brand. A brand such as Acura, for example may want to become part of a subcategory represented by Lexus. The task would be to convince customers that the subcategory should include cars that meet certain performance levels and that brands with a lower price point should not be excluded. Changing the subcategory definition may be a more effective strategy than convincing customers that Acura is superior to Lexus. Once a customer will accept the subcategory reframing so that Acura is relevant, the advantages of Acura will become evident.

Kraft's DiGiorno introduced a "rising crust" pizza, the first frozen pizza without a precooked crust, and reframed the frozen pizza subcategory to include delivered pizza. With the tagline "It's not delivery, it's DiGiorno," the strategy was a market success. The symbol of the reframed subcategory was the DiGiorno delivery person who, of course, has nothing to do because you don't need delivery for frozen pizza. In the reframed subcategory, DiGiorno, instead of being a premium-priced frozen pizza, now had a decided price advantage by being sometimes half the price of delivered pizza. Further, since it is a member of the broadened subcategory, its quality could be assumed to be comparable to delivered pizza.

CHANGING THE PERSPECTIVE AND VOCABULARY TOWARD THE SUBCATEGORY

The framing process works by shaping the choice discussion, providing a perspective and vocabulary that will enhance the chances that the new subcategory will find success. If the subcategory wins, so will the brand that is defining it.

A brand competing with Apple will have styling in the decision discussion. A competitor brand will have to explain that it has parity or superiority in design or why design should not be a deciding factor because the frame has elevated design to provide the initial perspective about the choice. A retailer who competes in the Whole Foods Market subcategory will have to show that understanding organic fresh food should not be a consideration and a skin care brand in the Dove subcategory will need to argue that moisturizer is not important. It will not be possible to ignore the framing structure because it is bigger than the brand. Each of the three brands has managed the buying decision so that a dimension into which they have the advantage is a part, if not the dominant part, of the purchase decision.

LAKOFF ON FRAMING

Framing a choice discussion was most clearly articulated by George Lakoff, an academic linguist from UC Berkeley, in his delightful book "Don't Think of an Elephant."[1] Lakoff, whose primary turf is political thinking, argues that Republicans are geniuses at framing and as a result win most of the arguments, while the clueless Democrats still think that rational thinking will carry the day. Republicans have framed discussions with terms like death taxes, partial-birth abortion, mandates, and tax relief. When their frame is accepted, the argument is over. Who would support a death tax?

Consider the difference in perspectives on taxation based on a phrase that frames the discussion. "Tax relief" engenders the metaphor of a hero who is relieving people of a burden with tax cuts. "Tax as investment in the future" produces the images of roads built, children educated, and a defense force enhanced. "Tax as dues" is a metaphor associated with paying your fair share for services benefiting you and others like you. Each frame influences the discourse and, very much like defining a subcategory, implicitly alters the objectives associated with choice. Republicans have made "tax relief" a winning frame.

Lakoff observes that frames are often cognitively unconscious in that people don't necessarily even realize that there is a frame or that the frame influences. That is in part why framing is so powerful. Further, a frame, once established, can linger. It is hard to change after being established. Lakoff likes to start off his Berkeley classes with the admonition to "not think of an elephant." Of course, students find it impossible to get the elephant out of their minds.

What makes one frame win? Finding the right label and/or metaphor to describe the frame that is on target and descriptive can be critical. It helps if it is a meaningful metaphor that will add visual imagery, memorability, and texture. Death taxes suggest the visual image of a casket surrounded by mourners. Tax relief has the metaphoric connotation that you will be relieved of a heavy, tired burden. The "good hands" of Allstate or the "good neighbors" of State Farm provide visual metaphors that serve to frame a subcategory.

And be persistent and disciplined. Always use the label or metaphor, never deviate. Make it so pervasive that competitors will also use it. That is when you know you have won.

A frame affects perceptions and preferences. A premium beer with some balsamic vinegar added, is preferred in taste tests unless the product is reframed as beer with vinegar added in which case it is perceived as disgusting.[2] A wine that was purported to be from California rather than North Dakota was not only preferred but caused users to linger over a meal.[3] The same wine! Just reframing a context in terms of positive instead of negative attributes can affect preferences. For example, people prefer 75 percent lean to 25 percent fat, even though the two choices are identical.[4]

Frames can actually dominate factual information. In a classic study, groups were shown two cameras, both described along five relevant dimensions.[5] The camera from the more impressive 35-mm single-lens reflex subcategory was preferred even with inferior specifications attached to it. Customers are either not motivated to take the time to learn about brands or actually lack the ability or background knowledge to do so. In either case, it is easier to rely on knowledge of what a frame stands for. An assumption that a brand is or is not relevant to a subcategory can dictate a person's perception and choice, and is hard to overcome.

Framing matters because it influences thinking, perceptions, attitudes, and behavior. The same information will be processed or not processed, be distorted or not distorted, affect attitudes and behavior or not affect attitudes and behavior, depending on the frame. It matters whether you are buying an energy bar for athletes, an energy bar for office workers, an energy bar for women, a nutrition bar, a breakfast bar, a protein bar, or a diet bar. In each case, the choice criteria and the perceptions of brands will be different.

BECOME THE EXEMPLAR OF THE SUBCATEGORY

The challenge is to manage the subcategory, to dictate its boundaries and control the perspective and vocabulary that is associated with it. The end goal is to influence perceptions, attitudes, and behavior toward the subcategory so that it wins the subcategory competition in the marketplace, and do it in such a way that "our" brand is the most relevant.

The best way to achieve that goal is to become the exemplar of the new subcategory, the brand that best represents it. For compact hybrids, the Prius defined the subcategory for over a decade. Jell-O, Gatorade, V8, Google, iPhone, Whole Foods Market, Enterprise Rent-A-Car, and Geek Squad are other examples of exemplars. A brand with a strong exemplar position can become the label for the subcategory. A customer will want to buy a "Prius"-type car or a "Kleenex"-type tissue.

If the brand is the exemplar, then it will, by definition, be the most visible and credible brand. Any competitors are in the awkward position of defining their relevance in a way that only reaffirms the authenticity and leadership of the exemplar.

With the exemplar status, the firm can control and evolve the subcategory frame and competitors will be on the defensive. In Chapter 7 it was noted that Gillette, Chrysler, and Apple, all playing the exemplar role, guided the evolution of a subcategory definition by adding models, improvements, and features to make it that much harder for competitors to become relevant.

How can a brand become an exemplar? Some guidelines:

First, advocate for the subcategory or category rather than the brand. Influence the image of the subcategory, attitudes toward it, and the role it plays in the life of customers. Use all of the same brand-building tactics and techniques that are used in brand building. Also, continue to innovate. Don't stand still. Innovation, improvement, and change will make the subcategory dynamic, the brand more interesting, and the role of the exemplar more valued. Disneyland is the exemplar of theme parks, and it is always innovating. Don't worry about the brand. If the category or subcategory wins, the brand will also win. Asahi Super Dry Beer, described in Chapter 7, was an advocate of dry beer, and when the subcategory won, Asahi Super Dry won.

Second, if possible, develop a descriptive label to help define the subcategory and be prepared to manage that label. Examples might be car sharing (Zipcar), fast fashion (Zara), high fiber (FiberOne), and healthy fast-food sandwiches (Subway). And then relentlessly use and manage that label. An ownable brand tagline can play a similar role. Consider some classics like de Beers' "A diamond is forever" that reframes diamonds from their functional benefits like sparkles to a symbol of a long-term love. Or "Melts in your mouth, not in your hand" that served to define an M&M subcategory for which other chocolates were not relevant. Beware that subcategory descriptions can be subtle. In an experiment, a firm that was framed as non-profit because of an .org suffix was perceived as more caring but less competent than a firm with a .com suffix.[6] Just the use of a web site suffix was enough to signal a different category of firms.

Third, invest to become the early market leader in terms of sales and market share. It is hard to both be an exemplar and leverage that role without market-share leadership. That means the brand will need to take risks to scale its operation to capture those customers that are attracted to the new "must have."

MAKE SURE THE SUBCATEGORY WINS

The ultimate job of the exemplar is to make sure that the subcategory wins. No brand does that better than Gillette. In India in 2008,

Gillette's premium shaving subcategory needed to fight the low-end, double-edged razors, that had a stubborn hold on 80 percent of the market, and a growing subcategory represented by men that shaved only once a week and were modeling the stubble look of some movie stars.

The breakthrough idea was Gillette's "Shave India Movement" designed to change perceptions and behavior toward the subcategory.[7] It was based in part on a 2008 Nielsen survey of women in India, which revealed that 77 percent of them preferred clean-shaven men. The effort involved the campaign, "India votes, to shave or not," the endorsement of two glamorous Bollywood actresses, the world-record-setting event in which 2,000 males shaved simultaneously, social media, infomercials, and more. The campaign got a boost in 2010 when Gillette sponsored W.A.L.S. (Women Against Lazy Stubble) with opinion polls, ads, and video clips in which female celebrities condemned stubble.

The momentum of the "Shave India Movement" helped, but new products were also needed especially to counter the low-end market. Into that context, Gillette made its signature Mach3 razor much less costly—from fifty times that of the double-edged razors to three times. Perhaps more important, the Gillette Guard, a razor equal in cost to the double edged razors, was developed. In addition, Gillette created a distribution strategy that accessed the rural retailers, which reach the mass of users outside urban areas.

By 2013 two out of every three razors sold in India was a Gillette Guard and the Mach3 enjoyed an increase in sales of some 500 percent.

The home-run program was subsequently imported into the United States as the Kiss & Tell campaign documenting the fact that women did not like stubble. A survey of 1,000 women found that one-third had actually avoided kissing a guy with facial hair. The campaign included a YouTube documentary (with a variety of experts relevant to kissing) a microsite (couples can provide kissing feedback at kissandtellus. com), and live events (the largest shaving lesson and the most kisses in one minute).

The take-away is that there is a huge pay-off in focusing on building and managing a subcategory and making it a winner rather than being preoccupied with "my brand is better than your brand" marketing.

THE BOTTOM LINE

Instead of promoting the superiority of the brand, consider framing a subcategory such that competitors are excluded or placed at a disadvantage. Strong frames can smother and distort rational information processing and dominate brand decisions. Becoming a subcategory exemplar, the best route of subcategory control, invokes selling the subcategory rather than the brand, creating and dominating a subcategory label, and becoming the perceived market leader. Making sure the subcategory wins is a route to brand growth.

PART III

Bring the
Brand to Life

Chapter 10

WHERE DO BRAND-BUILDING IDEAS COME FROM?

The best way to a good idea is to have lots to choose from.
—Linus Pauling

The quality of brand-building ideas and programs is, in most contexts, several times more important than the often fought-over budget levels. There is ample anecdotal and experimental evidence to support that assertion. One implication is to expend resources on finding truly effective brand-building initiatives. Another is to implement an effective test-and-learn system so that great initiatives can be detected and refined. A third is that when a big idea is found and developed, don't let go of it but, rather, keep it fresh and alive (see the discussion on program continuity in Chapter 13).

Creative brand-building ideas can come from anywhere, but there are some methods and perspectives that have been shown to be helpful at uncovering them. A few of these stand out:

• External role models
• Brand touchpoints

- Customer motivations and unmet needs
- Being opportunistic
- Leveraging assets
- Customer sweet spots

EXTERNAL ROLE MODELS

When I am asked for guidance for any brand or marketing problem, my response to most of these requests is that I know a method that is "guaranteed" to work. Find an organization that has successfully addressed a similar problem and adapt what they did. And don't limit the search to those organizations that look like your own, but be willing to look more broadly.

In this case the goal is to bring a core brand vision element to life. Your brand may aspire to be perceived as a systems-solution supplier, approachable, sustainable, global, or whatever. Reviewing a broad spectrum of product categories, identify a set of brands that focus on the same or similar core brand vision dimensions. Some fundamental questions should guide the search. What brands do you admire as having achieved the perceptions you aspire to have? Which of these brands represent best the interpretation of the brand vision element that your brand is striving for? Which were effective at communicating the vision?

With an external role model identified, the next step is to learn as much as possible from it. How did it achieve its perceptions? How did it develop authenticity and credibility? What are its stories? Proof points? What is its culture? What brand-building programs broke out of the clutter? Can any of their programs be modified to forward your brand's vision? The process represents the essence of creative thinking. Let ideas surface from different perspectives (the broader the better) and then work to refine and select.

Innovation, for example, is a core brand vision element for 3M, P&G, L'Oreal, Apple, Caterpillar, and Williams-Sonoma. What can each learn from the others? How can effective drivers of their image be applied in another brand context? Finding role models almost always leads to fresh thinking and insights.

A retail bank with a broad array of financial services that aspires to provide a trusted adviser role might look to Home Depot as a role model. Home Depot carries a wide variety of merchandise, has an approachable, friendly face, and helps customers with knowledge and substance. Customers can get professional help from someone who is not pretentious. When the bank's vision is framed in terms of Home Depot, its vision becomes more vivid. Another bank seeking to provide customers with a team capable of delivering an array of financial services might look to the ad agency Y&R, which delivers communication services using multi-functional, virtual teams organized around clients.

It is helpful not only to identify external role models that are on-strategy, but also to probe the boundaries—role models that are either "too much" or "not enough." A department store felt it needed to add energy to compete with specialty stores. The question was, what level of energy? A spectrum was conceived and retailer brands were positioned on the spectrum from boring (7-Eleven, CVS) to pleasant (Macy's, Pizza Hut) to delighted (Saks, Uniqlo) to excited (In & Out Burger, Urban Outfitters) to Wow (Niketown, Victoria's Secret). With that perspective, "excited" seemed the appropriate level, although insights came from role models at all levels. The concept of positioning role models on a scale was extremely useful in developing programs—like a sporting goods section with a host of hands-on demonstrations and a fashion section with a presentation that had real flare.

BRAND TOUCHPOINTS

The brand experience is at the essence of a relationship. It should be pleasant, exceed expectations, be on brand, and even inspire people to talk about positive interactions. It should not be frustrating or disappointing, and certainly should not motivate people to discuss negative incidents. Excelling on the brand experience can become a differentiating part of the value propositions. That was true for Staples, which created the "easy" in-store experience that affected a host of in-store touchpoints.

The brand experience is created by brand touchpoints that occur any time a person in the marketplace interacts with the brand. All touchpoints do not have the same impact, the same weakness in execution, or the same cost structure. Prioritizing and upgrading the touchpoints can be done using a five step process.[1]

1. **Identify all existing and potential touchpoints**. Touchpoints can be controlled by the organization, but can also be directed

by another entity, like a retailer or a social media vehicle. Be sure to consider touchpoints that are candidates to be added.

2. **Evaluate the touchpoint experience**. For which touchpoints are internal expectations not being met? What will it take in terms of resources and program change to improve the experience or to add a needed new touchpoint experience? How does it compare with the ideal experience? Make sure that all the segments are covered. At Jiffy Lube the experience was designed by men for men, yet 70 percent of the customers were women, who had a different take on the brand touchpoints.

3. **Determine the impact of each touchpoint on customer decisions and attitudes**. Which are the ones that really matter, that influence the relationship going forward?

4. **Prioritize**. A high-priority touchpoint would have a deficient experience, influence the customer relationship, and have a cost-efficient fix.

5. **Develop an action plan**. For the priority touchpoints, develop a program to change the touchpoint experience. Identify who is responsible for the change initiative and how the improvement should be measured.

The first three steps can be facilitated with RET (real-time experience tracking) whereby a respondent is given an app that allows him or her to note and evaluate each touchpoint experience by addressing four questions: 1) Which of a small set of brands was involved? 2) Which type of touchpoint was experienced from a provided list? 3) How positive did the experience make you feel? 4) Given the experience, how much more likely are you to choose the brand?[2] RET allows touchpoints and their impact to be quantified without following people around or relying on their memory.

From Touchpoints to Journeys

Improving the brand experience at every touchpoint is one way to build and solidify brand relationships. However, a bigger idea is to consider a journey—a set of touchpoints that are activated in response to a motivating customer task, issue, or problem.[3] For example, a customer may need to obtain information on offerings, start or change a service, or solve a technical problem. In each case there may be several touchpoints involved, perhaps from different organizational units.

With a journey perspective, the goal is to make the entire journey simple, easy, understandable, and efficient. Instead of improving the experience associated with a touchpoint, there might be elimination or consolidation of touchpoints. There might be a better hand-off from one touchpoint to the next. Or an examination of some root causes of dissatisfaction may result in the journey being completely reformulated or eliminated. The five step process may still work, but at the level of journey instead of touchpoints.

CUSTOMER MOTIVATIONS AND UNMET NEEDS

The customer and potential customers, and their use of the offering, can be a source of ideas. The most direct way to uncover them is to ask customers to identify motivations, problems, and unmet needs. The result may turn out to be subtle and a springboard to a brand-building program. Customer problems with buying a car led Lexus to create a buying experience that is more supportive and informative. Best Buy developed the Geek Squad, which helps customer install and service home entertainment and computer systems, in response to customer dissatisfaction.

However, customers may not be able or willing to provide insights. Henry Ford was famously quoted as saying that if you asked customers about their transportation unmet needs, they would have said "faster horses." And sometimes customers may be reluctant to show their superficiality and incorrectly claim they buy solely on functionality.

One research technique that addresses that problem, anthropological research, involves "living with" and observing customers as they shop for or use brands to learn about their habits, processes, and problems. P&G, committed to such research, had a group of its marketers "live" with Mexican lower-income families.[4] P&G researchers found that providing clean clothes was a priority, that laundry was time consuming, that 90 percent used softeners, that several rinse cycles were involved, and that water shortage was a critical problem. As a result, P&G created Downey Single Rinse, which directly addressed not only the water shortage but the time involved; it was a huge success.

The anthropological approach works in BtoB settings as well. The financial data company, Thomson, analyzed the time three minutes before and three minutes after their data was used.[5] They found that customers were inputting the data into spreadsheets and were able to create a service that eliminated that step, thereby improving the value proposition. This research is time-intensive but can be made more efficient by having respondents record and comment on their thoughts and experiences in real time, online, using a smartphone.

Brand teams can bypass customers entirely and make judgments on motivation and unmet needs by analyzing the customer context and by making judgments about how it could be improved. Certainly customers could not have imagined the option of buying products in a dedicated Apple store, with its energy, clean layout, and Genius Bar. Yet Steve Jobs had the insight that such a store would present the essence of the Apple brand and would be welcomed by customers.

BEING OPPORTUNISTIC

The best brand builders are opportunistic. When Hyundai won the coveted 2009 Car of the Year award from the North American International Auto Show, it was able to exploit that award by providing credibility (with an explanation point) to its quality and styling story. A brand-building team needs to be nimble and flexible in order to leverage such opportunities.

Korea in 2011 was involved in a president-driven country brand-building effort managed by a high-level council. The council tended to focus on taglines (one member told me that if the right tagline was found, success would follow), visuals, local events, and modest advertising. My take was that they should instead leverage off of events, firms, and people. For example, when Korea was the site of the World Cup in 2010, they should use that to advance the Korea brand. When Korea hosts their annual Korean Knowledge Forum, which brings in thought leaders from all over the world, the council should find ways to tell their story in that context, where the exposure and impact will be huge. And when a Korean woman, So Yeon Ryu, wins the U.S. Open Golf Championship, supplying a coach to help her handle the winning moment and afterglow, and to make sure she makes her national background a part of her story, will pay off and cost a fraction of any advertising effort.

LEVERAGING ASSETS

A brand does not have to build a program from the ground up. Rather, it can build on its assets.

Returning to the Korean story—the brand-building council will have a modest budget to be used for advertising and events. At the same time, Samsung and Hyundai will spend well over $1.5 billion in media advertising in the United States alone and many times that in terms of their global marketing budget. If only a small part of that budget could go to advance the Korea brand agenda, it would dwarf any council effort. The reality is that the image of a nation is driven by the image of its largest firms. Think of the impact of Singapore Airlines on Singapore, or Mercedes on Germany.

Another asset is established symbols. For countries there is the Guggenheim at Bilbao, the Edinburgh castle, and trekking in Nepal. For brands, there is the Wells Fargo stage coach, the Budweiser Clydesdales, the Disney characters, Betty Crocker, and on and on. When an iconic symbol is available, particularly when it tells a brand story by itself, it should be leveraged.

CUSTOMER SWEET SPOTS

Brand building is about communicating the brand and its vision to customers. A very different approach is to make the brand an active partner in an area that the customer is interested in or even passionate about. Chapter 11 will explore why that option can be effective and how to implement it.

MORE

These six approaches work, almost guaranteed. However, there are many other approaches that can be helpful, such as:

- Use the **creative thinking** discipline targeted at specific brand-building arenas. Effective creative thinking sessions should have a clear objective, avoid any evaluation during the process of coming up with ideas or improving them, and employ lateral thinking (start the process from different, even outlandish points of reference). In general, creativity is aided by breaking the routine, perhaps by going on a field trip to gain new perspectives.

- **Find and leverage stories** about customer experiences, employee actions, or the early days of the organization. The story about how Thomas Edison founded GE in 1890—based on a set of inventions that involving lighting, transportation, power, and medical equipment—bring today's GE alive. Stories work by making any message more vivid, authentic, and memorable. Story power is discuss in Chapter 14 in the context of internal branding, but it can apply to external brand-building as well.

- **Empower all units in the organization** to come up with ideas. A great brand idea can come from another country, from another product class that carries the brand, from the digital team, or from sponsorship initiatives. Pantene's "Hair So Healthy It Shines" came from Taiwan, Nestlé's ice cream snack Dibs came from the U.S., and Levi's Dockers came from South America. The key is to not only stimulate ideas but also to test, leverage, and scale the outstanding ideas quickly. Chapter 20, which discusses the silo problem, elaborates.

- **Employ crowdsourcing**. Pose a question, such as designing a promotion or event that engages a target audience, to participants of one of the many crowdsourcing sites. Keys to effectiveness include having a well defined brief, an attractive incentive to participate, and a way to evaluate the inputs.

- Look at **competitor weaknesses,** even for potential "reasons not to buy," and attempt to position them as well as your brand. When PowerBar introduced Pria in response to Clif Bar's Luna (the first women's energy bar), Pria was able to message around being more petite, having fewer calories, and having a different and better taste and texture.

- Examine **emerging applications or market segments,** because they might provide a pathway not only to growth, but to freshening the brand. Recall the classic finding that Arm & Hammer baking soda could de-odorize a refrigerator. It forever changed the brand.

- **Refine, refine, refine.** Great brand-building programs do not appear on the scene in final polished form. Rather, a potential idea will need to evolve over time, changing and improving until a great idea emerges. Further, its implementation will usually require a series of test-and-learn steps.

THE BOTTOM LINE

Don't be satisfied with spending a brand-building budget. Rather seek breakthrough ideas. Ideas can come from anywhere, but can be facilitated by a host of methods and processes such as exploring external role models, analyzing brand touchpoints, identifying customer motivations and unmet needs, leveraging assets, being opportunistic. What is as important is the willingness to invest behind the brand vision, the motivation to bring it to life, and the aspiration to create "big" brand-building ideas.

Chapter 11

FOCUS ON CUSTOMER'S SWEET SPOTS[1]

*It is useless to tell a river to stop running: the best thing
is to learn how to swim in the direction it is flowing.*
—**Anonymous**

The instinct when creating a marketing strategy is to ask: how can the offering, brand, and firm be advanced? How can visibility be enhanced, associations reinforced, and user loyalty increased? This orientation is driven by financial performance goals and by the assumption that customers are rational and will want to know and act on information regarding a product or service. The problem is that offering-driven brand-building and marketing is often ineffective because it does not engage customers, especially when the offering is inconsequential within, tangential to, or detached from their lifestyle. That is especially true with digital strategies that hope to activate a community.

There is an alternative. Look for a customer "sweet spot" and find a "shared interest" idea or program that will involve connecting the brand with that sweet spot. A sweet spot—whether it be New York City adventures, healthy living, rock climbing, sustainability, or a college football team—should be related to what is important and involving to customers; what they are motivated to talk about. Ideally, it would be a part of, if not central to, their self-identity and lifestyle and/or reflect a higher-order purpose in their lives.

The shared-interest program can be formed around the offering or brand, especially for a high-involvement brand like Tesla or Xbox. However, for most brands and firms, offerings are not relevant to any potential customer sweet spot. In that case, an event, activity, interest area, or cause needs to be created or found that does connect to a true customer sweet spot. It needs to resonate, break out of the clutter, and provide a hub around which a set of coordinated brand-building programs can be developed. Consider Pampers and Coke, for example, plus the Dove "Campaign for Real Beauty" story described below.

Pampers went beyond diapers by "owning" the website Pampers Village, which provides a go-to place for all issues relating to babies and child care and gets more than 600,000 unique visitors each month. Its seven sections—Pregnancy, New Baby, Baby Development, Baby Toddler, Preschool, Me, and Family—all have a menu of topics. For example, under "Baby Development" there are 57 articles, 230 forums, and 23 play-and-learn activities. Its online community allows moms and soon-to-be moms to connect with each other to share their common experiences and thoughts about how to raise a healthy, happy child. The program demonstrates that Pampers understands mothers, and works to establish a relationship between the brand and the mother that will potentially continue throughout the mother's Pampers-buying life.

Coca-Cola exhibited a higher purpose by partnering with the World Wildlife Foundation, which is engaged in major initiatives to conserve water, reduce carbon emissions, and save polar bears. A visible Coke component is an effort to spotlight the polar bears with research (customers can contribute and receive a virtual piece of arctic land from which they can monitor bears) and promotions such as the Polar Pick-me-up, where a person can send a Coke to a friend. The Coke Facebook site, with 35 million "likes," coordinates the effort. The community provides Coke with likability, energy, and customer engagement. It will resonate with a segment important to Coke that is likely to be different than the segment that responds to the humorous videos around Coke "happiness."

DOVE: CAMPAIGN FOR REAL BEAUTY

Dove's "Campaign for Real Beauty," originated in Brazil by Ogilvy & Mather in 2004, set out to make women aware that they have real beauty that is not based on a standard of a young, model-thin body with excessive make-up. The goal was to make a fundamental change in the way women are perceived and in their self-esteem. The campaign started with advertisements showing real women who may have been older or heavier than the "ideal," but exhibited beauty. Billboard ads invited passers-by to vote on whether a particular model was, for example, "Fat or Fab" or "Wrinkled or Wonderful," with the results of the votes dynamically updated.

In one campaign variant, a forensic sketch artist drew several women first based only on their descriptions of themselves (he does not actually see them) and then based on the descriptions of a stranger who has observed the women. The subject, seeing the resulting sketches side-by-side, realizes that the sketches inspired by strangers are much more flattering than the versions from their own self-descriptions. The tagline? "You are more beautiful than you think." The first two three-minute Dove Real Beauty Sketch ads each got over 35 million viewers within two weeks after being posted on YouTube.

The "Real Beauty" campaign involves substantive programs, with girls as one prominent target. Dove has collaborated with Girl Scouts of the USA to promote self-esteem and leadership programming among tween and teenage girls with programs like "Uniquely ME!" and "It's Your Story—Tell It!" An annual Dove Self-Esteem Weekend aims to inspire moms and mentors to talk to girls in their lives about beauty, confidence, and self-esteem, supported by discussion aids.

The Real Beauty campaign resonated at several levels. It connected with an issue of deep concern with the customer base—their own appearance and self-confidence. Additionally, it addressed the insecurity and self-esteem issues of young women with which customers could empathize. It struck a chord. It provided a higher purpose to the brand and a shared interest with customers.

The impact in equivalent measured media for some of its efforts has been estimated to be thirty times their expenditures. One of its ads, Evolution, which showed how much effort goes behind creating what is an "artificial model look," won advertising awards and created unpaid exposure estimated to be worth more than $150 million. There are anecdotes about dramatic sales increases tied to the campaign, and surveys showing that those aware of the effort are more likely to use and recommend Dove products. But the creation of a huge business base estimated to exceed $3 billion is the best evidence of its impact.

The Dove brand success did not just happen. It was research-based, with a host of methods employed to understand the issues women face with respect to Dove products and perceived beauty. Customer research was supplemented with expert guidance. The Dove Self-Esteem Program, for example, has an eleven person Global Advisory Board. There is also an ability and willingness to stimulate and then access creative thinking from around the world, and then push the best ideas into the marketplace. Letting ideas emerge and then flourish is not a natural part of most organizations. Dove's efforts are remarkable.

WHAT DOES A CUSTOMER-DRIVEN SWEET-SPOT PROGRAM BUY?

To connect with a customer sweet spot provides avenues to a relationship much richer than that of an offering-based relationship that, for most brands, is driven by a functional benefit and is relatively shallow and vulnerable. In particular, a sweet-spot program can potentially:

Create Brand Energy and Interest

One of the key challenges for most brands globally is to create energy and visibility. For Avon, for example, the product line is not an energy source, but the Avon Walk for Breast Cancer creates involvement, connects to an area the target audience has passion about, and attaches a higher purpose to the Avon brand. Millions of women have participated directly or indirectly over two decades and are proud that the program has raised more than $600 million for cancer research. That is energy.

If you make hot dogs it is hard to manufacture energy. However, if you focus on the events and parties so important to kids and create the Oscar Meyer Wienermobile (or more accurately eight of them) and add a jingle contest, you have real energy. No amount of product innovation around hot dogs could come close.

Enhance Brand Likability and Credibility

Connecting a brand to a customer sweet spot raises the brand way above the noise emanating from firms shouting "my brand is better than your brand." The positive feelings associated with the shared-interest area can lead to positive feelings about the brand—people attribute all sorts of good characteristics to liked brands with whom they share interests.

Hobart, a maker of high-end institutional kitchen equipment, became a thought leader and information source in regard to such issues as finding, training, and retaining good workers; keeping food safe; providing enticing dining experiences; eliminating costs; and reducing shrinkage. Hobart became the firm with "Good Equipment, Good Advice." This program impacted perceptions of and attitudes toward the brand and propelled Hobart into a leadership role that lasted well over a decade, until they were bought and integrated into a larger firm.

The hypothesis that there will be an image boost from a positive, involving shared-interest program is supported by the halo effect, first studied in the 1930s by the psychologist Edward Thorndike in the context of the impact of a person's attractiveness on perceptions of other characteristics. When applied to brands and marketing, it suggests that one brand association will influence perceptions of other associations. It helps explain the positive impact of celebrity endorsers, why successful brand extensions enhance a brand image, and why a brand's credible involvement in a shared interest will affect the brand's likability and image. A person will tend to regard favorably an entity that shares his or her values and interests.

Form a Friend, Colleague, or Mentor Brand Relationship

The existence of a sweet-spot program makes a friend, colleague, or mentor relationship metaphor likely to be applicable.[2] California Casualty, an auto and home insurance firm that specializes in teachers, has a "School Lounge Makeover" program to provide $7,500 to upgrade teacher lounges for schools with a compelling story. Only a friend would take an interest in such a mundane but important issue area. California Casualty also acts as a colleague, sharing goals and programs by being a sponsor and partner in IMPACT, an organization that is designed to address teenage distracted driving through in-school educational and involvement programs. Finally, the brand can be like a mentor. General Mills, who shares an interest in gluten-free living with its website GlutenFreely.com, for example, is in a position to support a community around gluten issues with advice and encouragement.

Stimulate a Social Network

A social community associated with a sweet-spot initiative often has the potential to have a high level of social activity, increasingly difficult to obtain in an era of social media fatigue. Focusing on what a person is passionate about such as baby care with Pampers Village or motorcycle trips on the Harley-Davidson site will motivate the user to reach out for information or to share experiences and ideas. It can stimulate the major reasons to be socially active—content involvement (gain or spread information that is especially intriguing or useful), self-involvement (gain attention, show knowledge), and other involvement (belonging to a community and helping others).

How to Proceed

Creating a successful shared-interest program, as suggested by Figure 4, involves identifying a customer sweet spot and then finding or creating a connecting program. Each step has substantial uncertainties and challenges.

IDENTIFY A SHARED INTEREST THAT WILL ENGAGE THE AUDIENCE

The first challenge is to find a set of potential sweet spots by understanding the customers in depth. How do they spend their quality time? What activities do they enjoy? What possessions are important to them and reflect their personality and lifestyle? What do they talk about?

What issues absorb their attention? In what areas do they hold strong opinions? What are their values and beliefs? Their higher purpose?

With an understanding of the customer in hand, there are three on-ramps to the identification of the right shared-interest program.

The Offering Is an Integral Part

The first on-ramp is to determine if the brand can be integrated into a "sweet-spot" program and be a full partner that contributes assets and substance. The health care organization, Kaiser Permanente, for example, repositioned its brand away from a focus on health care (linked to bureaucracy and sickness) to a shared interest in healthy lifestyles (associated with control and wellness). The shared-interest program involves members controlling their own health by accessing a wide array of preventive health programs addressing areas such as weight control, stress management, insomnia, smoking issues, healthy eating, and many others, all supported by "My Health Manager," which can be used to record and monitor program participation. These programs have their own focus and objectives, which are very different from selling compassionate staff and clean, effective hospitals.

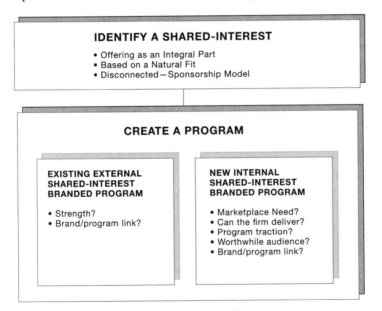

IDENTIFY A SHARED-INTEREST
- Offering as an Integral Part
- Based on a Natural Fit
- Disconnected—Sponsorship Model

CREATE A PROGRAM

EXISTING EXTERNAL SHARED-INTEREST BRANDED PROGRAM
- Strength?
- Brand/program link?

NEW INTERNAL SHARED-INTEREST BRANDED PROGRAM
- Marketplace Need?
- Can the firm deliver?
- Program traction?
- Worthwhile audience?
- Brand/program link?

A Shared-Interest Program
Figure 4

A Fit Based On a Natural Association

A second on-ramp is to build on a sweet spot that has a natural connection to the brand. There are a host of bases for a brand connection such as a lifestyle (Zipcars and urban-lifestyle living), an offering application (Harley-Davidson and touring on motorcycles), an activity (Adidas Streetball Challenge—a local three-person basketball tournament surrounded by a weekend party with music, dancing, etc.), a target customer (Pampers and baby care), a country (Hyundai makes and sponsors the Kimchi Bus, a 400-day effort to spread Korean cuisine), values (Dove on redefining beauty), or an interest (the Sephora BeautyTalk site for those interested in beauty tips and issues). The fit should work—it should not be incongruous.

Disconnected—Sponsorship Only

A third on-ramp is to find or create a sweet-spot program that has no connection or a remote connection. The Avon Walk for Breast Cancer has little relationship with its offerings. Nor do many of the events connect to the energy drink, Red Bull, including the Red Bull Air Race, for example. Relaxing the commonly held dictum that there must be some kind of brand fit or connection means that the search for a sweet-spot area that customers will be truly involved with will be unconstrained. Anything is eligible and thus a winning idea is more likely. However, linking the brand to a disconnected program can then become a challenge.

CREATE AN INTERNAL SHARED-INTEREST SWEET-SPOT PROGRAM

An internal, owned, shared-interest program, such as the Pampers Village or Avon's Walk for Breast Cancer, has compelling advantages. In particular, the substance, evolution, and investment can be controlled by the firm. However, the cost and difficulty of establishing a new program can be formidable. Thus, the likely feasibility and success of the programs should be tested with five questions.

1. **Is there a need for a new shared-interest program?** The more attractive a shared-interest area is, the more likely that others have already entered. These entrants may not be competitor brands but other organizations. The top recipe brands FoodNetwork.com and Allrecipes.com, with impressive content and strong brands, are controlled by media companies rather than food brands. A key question—can the existing efforts be either surpassed with something superior or neutralized with a niche strategy that is more focused? Is there room for another effort? What is missing? There needs to be an opportunity for a new entrant.

2. **Can the firm deliver?** A shared-interest program needs to have real substance that is in some way unique, whether it is in content or presentation. There will have to be assets and competences developed or outsourced. Organizational support for an extended time period in which there will be setbacks and competing uses of resources will also be needed.

3. **Can the program get traction?** A shared-interest program will need enough visibility and credibility to be considered by target group members. It has to be relevant. The task is made easier if a brand's existing assets, such as a well-trafficked website, can be leveraged. The Sephora site, for example, had a significant flow of customers that provided a base audience for the shared-interest BeautyTalk sub-site (which offers "real-time answers, expert advice, access to a community, and your fix to all things beauty"), in addition to the credibility provided by the Sephora brand. The program also needs to find a way to be sticky (to be used on a regular basis) by making sure the content is fresh and that involvement is enabled and encouraged.

4. **Is the audience size worthwhile?** The ultimate audience size needs to be meaningful to the business. Raw numbers, however, are not the only criteria. The quality of the audience counts as much as its quantity. In fact, there is a saying that it is better to be loved by a few than liked by many.

5. **Can the brand connect to the program?** If the brand is to be enhanced by the program, the two need to be linked. If the program shares the brand name, the link will usually be in place, but the credibility and authenticity of the program may be challenged. If the program does not include the brand name, a plan is needed to make sure that the link is developed.

FIND AN EXISTING EXTERNAL PROGRAM

The classic make-or-buy decision should be on the table. An internal, owned, sweet-spot program means that the substance, evolution, and investment can be controlled by the firm. However, establishing a new program can be costly, difficult, and even not feasible, especially if the sweet-spot program candidates have been already preempted in the marketplace or if the firm lacks the resources to create a competing program.

An option is to find an established, branded sweet-spot program with proven visibility and effectiveness and link to it. Home Depot wanted a program to leverage its assets and expertise to help the disadvantaged to build or re-build homes. The solution was to connect to Habitat for Humanity, a branded program with an established record of success in building homes for those that need help. Home Depot provided visible and tangible support with building supplies, volunteers from its knowledgeable staff, and signage in stores and on its website. For many customers of Home Depot, the link was well-known. As an aside, it does not matter if Habitat for Humanity is linked to Home Depot, only the reverse, because the goal is to influence the Home Depot brand.

THE BOTTOM LINE

Customers are not interested in efforts to promote an offering, brand, or firm, yet that is the basis of much marketing. An alternative is to focus on the activities or interests that customers *are* involved with, their sweet spot. The challenge is to create a sweet-spot program in which the brand is seen as a shared-interest partner. It is a big idea and can result in providing the brand with energy, likability, and credibility; the basis for a deeper relationship; and an activated social network. There are three on-ramps to a shared-interest program depending on whether the offering is embedded into the program, linked to it, or independent of it. The cost and evolution of an internal, owned program can be controlled by the organization, but an external program with an established brand and record will sometimes be more effective and feasible.

Chapter 12

DIGITAL—A CRITICAL BRAND-BUILDING TOOL

It is kind of fun to do the impossible.
—**Walt Disney**

D igital capability involving websites, blogging, social media, online video, the smart phone world, and more has become a necessity for organizations that want to build or enhance their brand and create breakthrough brand programs. Digital is a particularly powerful force for brands and brand building because it:

- **Engages**. Digital programs, especially those that involve a community, often stimulate comments and recommendations. An engaged audience will be susceptible to listening, learning, believing, and behavior change as compared to having only passive exposures to an advertisement or seeing the name of a sponsor at an event. Passive exposure is a tough route to communication and attitude change.
- **Allows content to be rich and deep**. Social media is not limiting in terms of content. A website can contain an enormous amount

of information, and a four-minute video can tell a story with depth.

- **Targets**. Most digital modalities can target even to the level of an individual. A visitor to a website, for example, can tailor the experience to his or her needs.
- **Garners trust**. Compared to paid media television or print ads, website content and online customer opinions have a higher level of trust because more content implies substance and because the "selling objective" is less apparent.[1]

Digital marshals these attributes and builds brands in four ways. As shown in Figure 5, it can augment the offering, support the offering, create brand-building platforms, or amplify other brand-building platforms.

AUGMENT THE OFFERING

A digital program can augment the offering, adding functional benefits. Consider Nike+, where a chip embedded in a shoe can provide a record of the athlete's activity. Some museums have an app that provides a convenient tour guide, thereby making the experience richer. NASCAR has an app that allows someone attending the race to listen to the conversation between drivers and the pit crew—they are now "insiders." Cabs in London and some other cities have an app that allows people to contact the closest cab and arrange a pickup. Some airlines have apps that allow fliers to check in, monitor flights, and change reservations. FedEx provides an app that allows customers to track their shipments. In all these cases, the digital program becomes part of the offering and enhances its value. It also adds to the perception that the brand has energy, is innovative, and is even creating "must haves" that define new subcategories.

SUPPORT THE OFFERING

Digital can support the offering by making it more understandable and credible and by making the purchase process less frustrating. It can also encourage new applications and provide a mechanism to improve the offering.

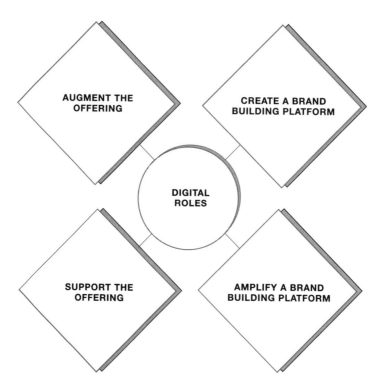

The Role of Digital
Figure 5

Communicate and Support the Offering

A very basic tool is having a website and other platforms, like Facebook that communicate the offering. A website can help a customer learn about an offering, especially when it is complex or dynamic. Subway, for example, communicates new and existing sandwiches, often in the context of a promotion. They have some 22 million Facebook followers, but more important than the number is the unusually high engagement. Visitors are looking for the new sandwich and promotion of the day. Walmart is a site that allows people to access product information and deals among a huge array of products. Their visitors have a high level of engagement because the site allows them to navigate a lot of information and get to what interests them at the moment. In each case, there is a functional reason to be involved and return.

Websites oriented around the offering, such as Subway and Walmart, need to be clean, easy to use, and designed with good navigation. The power of simplicity is shown by its effect on customer decisions. A study published in the *Harvard Business Review* found that those brands that scored in the top quarter on delivering simple, relevant information were 86 percent more likely to be purchased and 115 percent more likely to be recommended to others.[2]

The power of digital support gets enhanced when customers can interact with the organization behind the brand or with other customers. Dell, for example, has a host of support forums with interactive dimensions, including owner's clubs, the venerable Direct2Dell, blogs around interest areas such as enterprise IT, and much more.

Provide Credibility to the Offering

The customer also wants trustworthy, relevant information about brands, and guidance as to how to compare them. Often, customer input based on actual experience without commercial bias is seen to deliver. Walt Disney World's Moms Panel, for example, answers questions about the Disney vacation. JC Penney posts videos of teens talking about their purchases (termed "hauls") and provides insights into what purchases were made and why. TurboTax provides more than 100,000 unfiltered reviews of their products and helps customers find the most relevant reviews for their needs.

Expert relevant commentary also is a route to credibility. Saks Fifth Avenue relies on expert commentary and has fashion writer Dana Riggs give fashion advice to its customers. Betty Crocker has an "Ask Betty" forum that provides the image of the heritage expert. The digital forms allow this advice to have a personal touch.

Help Make the Purchase Process Easier

When customers search for brand information they often will welcome some help with the decision process. They may be frustrated and confused with product information that is not in a format that is easy to use. Several automobile brands, recognizing that reality, offer the ability to compare their brand to other relevant brands and become the setting for decision making.

Anything that can reduce the complexity of a decision will be welcome. DeBeers uses the 4 Cs (cut, color, clarity, and carat) to frame a complex decision and express its leadership status. Information that is screened for relevance will be valued. Herbal Essences provides a decision guide based on identifying hair type and color treatment needs that simplifies the hair-treatment decision. ShoeDazzle.com provides shoe suggestions based on personality information such as favorite fashion icons and heel preference.

Encourage Applications

A key to growth can be to find new applications for the brand and then to encourage their use. As noted in Chapter 8, Harley-Davidson has a website on which users post their favorite rides, complete with maps and high points. Home Depot utilizes different social media vehicles and their website to get customers to think about home improvements. Cosmetic firms explain how and when to use their products. Such efforts would be difficult to implement without digital capabilities.

Engage the Customer in Product Development and Evaluation.

An area of customer interaction that is a win-win is to get them to provide and evaluate ideas for new or improved offerings. MyStarbucksIdea, started in 2008, has changed Starbucks. Splash sticks to protect consumers from hot drink spills, mobile payments, new flavors including skinny beverages, and cake pop treats all came out of the site. Not all ideas, (like separate lines for brewed coffee) work out, but even those provide vitality and connection to the brand. Heineken has reached 11 million Facebook fans (over three times that of Budweiser), in part because of its bottle redesign challenge. The first annual contest to design the next limited-edition bottle received more than 30,000 entrants. The ideas implemented by these brands may not be as important has having on ongoing dialogue with customers and providing employees with first hand customer contact.

CREATE A BRAND-BUILDING PLATFORM

Digital brand-building platforms can play a central role, or even be a lead modality, with other marketing efforts playing a supporting role. Singapore Airlines, for example, sponsored a video contest in which participants submitted a video of their favorite vacation sites in Asia. Winners received airline tickets and a stay at a four-star hotel. ESPN apps allow fans to check scores and stats in real time. In both cases, these are brand-building platforms that are supported by other modalities.

A brand-building platform is often based on finding and becoming a focal point for a customer sweet spot. In Chapter 10, several examples of website-driven brand-building platforms, which stimulated the involvement of a community, were presented, such as:

- The Pampers Village web site that became a go-to place for all things around baby care.
- Hobart's effort to be the thought leader and information source for the customers of its institutional kitchen appliance line, which included white papers posted on its website.
- Sephora's BeautyTalk, the place for all things beauty.

Online Viral Videos

A successful online video can be a brand-building platform. Not easy to achieve, but when it clicks, it can stimulate quality exposures and engage the target audience, often at a fraction of the cost of paid media. DC Shoes, a maker of footwear and other products with a focus on skateboarders and snowboarders, started in 2009 with videos showing a stunt driver around familiar settings like the streets of San Francisco. Over four years they have earned 180 million views, worth at least $5 million in paid online media.[3]

And there was the Coke "Happiness Machine," the video of which was seen by more than 10 million consumers. At a student hangout at St. John's University, a person bought a Coke from a "Happiness Machine" and got not just one Coke but, to her surprise, a stream of them. Then a hand emerged with flowers, followed by a Coke plus a glass full of ice, a balloon dog, a pizza, and finally, a submarine sandwich yards long. A lot of laughter ensued and one student tried to hug the machine.

Social Media-Driven Promotions

Digital enables firms to conduct promotions that would not otherwise have been feasible. In 2009, Ford Fiesta wanted to create awareness and consideration among millennials for a 2011 model based on a European design. The solution was to place a hundred cars in the hands of a hundred digitally vibrant "influentials" across the country. During each month of the half-year program, each "agent" completed a theme mission that Ford devised and described their experience and thoughts via video, tweets, blog posts, etc. The program received a half-billion impressions, a brand awareness of more than 40 percent, and thousands of pre-orders—all with no media advertising.

The promotion became an annual effort known as "The Next Fiesta Movement" with a hundred "influentials" each year selected. One twist is that the social-media-based program leverages its output by using it in Fiesta advertising. Another twist is the use of two comedians, selected via a vote among consumers, who ride around Los Angeles in a Fiesta and compete to perform the best impromptu stand-up comedy in front of random audiences, with the content promoted on YouTube and elsewhere.

AMPLIFYING BRAND-BUILDING PROGRAMS

Digital is well-suited to amplify other brand-building initiatives; it just makes all elements of brand-building programs work harder and be more effective. In particular, the website can be a central node, enhancing just about all brand-building platforms from sponsorships and media advertising to promotions, events, and more. Mobile apps leverage programs to the smart phone space. Social media outlets such as Twitter and e-mail newsletters can drive people to events and make sponsorships visible. Breakthrough advertising can have an extended life in the social media world.

To illustrate, consider how sponsorships benefit from supporting digital activity.

Support and Enhance a Sponsorship.

Think about how digital amplifies the Avon Walk for Breast Cancer. The website is a place where participants, their friends, and supporters can find out about the race, the schedule, the process of participating, and how to donate. And a NASCAR sponsor can amplify its association with NASCAR and support promotions with an involving and informative website.

Digital amplifies the sponsorships of Red Bull, the high-caffeine energy soda, which has created or sponsored hundreds of events and competitions each year. The home run was in 2012, when well over eight million watched digitally while Felix Baumgartner rose more than twenty-four miles above the New Mexico desert in the fifty-five-story, ultra-thin helium "Red Bull Stratos" balloon, jumped off, and reached 830 mph during a nine-minute fall. Since then another 40 million have seen the YouTube video alone. The pre-jump and post-jump digital activity plus documentaries have totaled more than a billion impressions, which meant an incredible ROI of the Red Bull investment, even at a price tag of over $40 million. The impact would have been a fraction of that without digital.

BUILDING OUT DIGITAL

Creating a sound, flexible digital capability is not easy. Some guidelines:

Achieve Capabilities with a Wide Range of Digital Modalities

Digital is not just one modality—it is a set of many, and they are synergistic. It is usually the interlinking combination of different modalities that make the numbers and influence become impactful. Leaving some out will reduce the total impact.

Learn to Integrate Digital into the Marketing Effort.

Digital is too often organizationally and conceptually treated as another marketing vehicle that is somehow autonomous. Firms instead need to integrate digital into the total brand-building and marketing effort. A key role for digital is to amplify programs and support offerings. The challenge is organizational as well as technical, working with marketing teams of all types and understanding how digital amplifies in each context. Adjustments may need to be made in organizational processes, structure, people, and culture. More on overcoming functional organizational silos in order to create integrated marketing communication (IMC) appears in Chapter 20.

Think Strategic as Well as Tactical

There is a tendency to view digital as tactical, which is appropriate to support the offer or amplify other brand-building programs. Don't forget the possibility of using digital to augment the offering in a way that expands the value proposition, or creates a brand-building platform that is driven by digital capabilities. In either case, the digital program can become strategic, which has implications as to how it is resourced and how it is evaluated.

Experiment

Digital is an avenue that allows and rewards experimentation. Ideas can be explored with small budgets. Multiple executions can be developed, some using crowd sourcing, and tested quickly and efficiently. Small niche audiences can be targeted that would not be possible with other vehicles. This small audience can sometimes be scaled to major segments.

Listen

The world of digital media is not controlled by the brand; anyone can initiate thoughts and issues about brands and brand experiences. The brand can get attacked, sometimes with false claims, and the brand team should be in a position to respond or at least know about it. It is imperative to be *in* the game, not sitting on the sidelines. Further, having an opportunity to have ongoing interactions with customers has a lot of upside. Many firms, such as Gatorade, have set up social media command centers where all comments related to the brand are tracked. Sentiments such as the number of positive comments for every negative one, can be instructive. Issues, whether false or true, can be detected as they emerge, and some damaging ones can be killed off before they get traction. Helpful stories, new applications, and ideas for new products can be harvested.

Be Opportunistic

While the brand vision provides guidance and discipline, the organization needs to be fast on its feet—adaptive. The digital world is fast-moving and the opportunities will emerge and recede with rapidity. When a new brand-building platform emerges, whether within or outside digital, the digital modalities need to be prepared to cluster like bees to honey.

Think Content

It is all about content. Just having a sound brand vision, digital capabilities, and a budget is not enough. Creative ideas that lead to breakout programs are needed. That often means more resources should be devoted to idea generation and more sources of ideas accessed. The Coke Happiness Machine, for example, started with an idea that came out of a brainstorming session. Others have used crowd-sourcing vehicles, introduced in Chapter 10, where participants respond to creative challenges.

Social media is fueled by content. Only if the content is entertaining, functional, furthers an agenda, or resonates with an interest area will it be transmitted. And consumers often generate much of social media content. Of 150 million views of Coca-Cola related content, fewer than 20 percent were generated by the firm.[4] An implication is that a brand should create content that will be spread by the social media world. Another is that when content does get created by the marketplace that is on-brand, its dissemination should be encouraged.

Set Objectives, Measurable if Possible

The objectives for a digital program need to be clear. Is it to generate sales, build awareness, generate energy, support an image, enhance loyalty, or promote advocacy? And how do you evaluate a program given that measurement is expensive, short-term results may not be relevant, and modalities such as advertising or sponsorships can affect outcomes? Nevertheless, having the objectives clearly in mind will help.

What *can* be evaluated is the ability of the program to generate impressions. However, impressions are passive and engagement measures, such as making comments, re-tweeting, "linking," or buying are more likely to be associated with ultimate objectives of furthering the brand and the strength of its customer base.

THE BOTTOM LINE

Digital engages, allows rich content, targets, and engenders trust. It builds brands by augmenting the offering, supporting the offering, created brand-building platforms, and/or amplifying other brand-building platforms. Success in digital will involve participating in a wide range of modalities, achieving integrated marketing communication, avoiding thinking that digital is only tactical, experimentation, listening programs, opportunism, great content, and measurement.

Chapter 13

CONSISTENCY WINS

A diamond is a piece of coal that stuck to the job.
—Thomas A. Edison

One of the most important decisions a brand strategist makes is to change the brand strategy or its execution. Making an unwise or ill-timed change could represent a setback to the brand and business. Conversely, when changing circumstances make adaptation an imperative, a failure to adjust the brand strategy or the execution could result in damage to the brand and the business. It is thus important to understand when a change is warranted and why the rationale needs to be objectively and thoroughly vented.

CHANGE MOTIVATIONS

Five motivations can trigger a need to change.

First, you have evidence that the existing brand strategy is poorly conceived or cannot be executed. Perhaps the wrong segment, value proposition, or application has been targeted. Or the value proposition is one that cannot be made compelling. It is wasteful and even dangerous to prolong a strategy that is misguided or incompetent. The brand and business will suffer and the advent of a better approach will be delayed. This signals a clear need to take the brand strategy in a different direction.

BUT—it is not always easy to determine when to give up on the strategy. Are short-term market performance indicators predictive of long-term success, or is patience needed? Further, might unsatisfactory performance and prospects be caused by an offering limitation or lack of innovation rather than a brand-strategy issue? Most businesses will struggle to grow in the absence of dramatic innovation. There is just too much market inertia. Or brand strategy might be blamed when execution is in fact the problem.

Second, the execution simply is not breaking through the clutter; it is not resonating. A more innovative and involving execution is needed to bring the strategy to life. A challenge, but usually feasible if a compelling value proposition exists and an execution team can deliver creative, punchy programs that will register in the marketplace.

BUT—the execution may be close and just needs to be tweaked, modified, or extended in order to work. Or the execution may just take more time to wear in and get traction. Further, a superior execution may not be feasible given the offering and value proposition. Trying new executions may simply be futile.

Third, there are fundamental changes in the marketplace and the assumptions that underlie the brand strategy and execution no longer hold. The customers have moved on. The strategy and its execution may be defensible but the target market is fading or the offering is less relevant. If fewer customers are buying fried chicken or SUVs or individual stocks, the brand might need to be repositioned and the execution redone. Consider, for example, the need for the Kentucky Fried Chicken brand to change its name to KFC and shift its position away from that of Colonel Sanders' fried chicken.

BUT—the apparent threat from a trend or competitor innovation may be short-lived, even if there is buzz behind it. Any number of market forces or innovations have sizzled and then fizzled. Electric razors were supposed to make safety razors obsolete when introduced in the 1930s, but that did not happen. Further, even when a threat is real, it is not clear that the brand strategy should change. The old strategy with a "stick to your knitting" philosophy that has worked well in the past may represent a better strategy than alternatives. Chapter 15 elaborates on how to respond to market threats.

Fourth, the business strategy might evolve or even change. Another segment might be added. For example, Gillette is now also for women, and Ford is serious about customers wanting smaller, less expensive cars. Or the brand might be extended. GE has moved into energy areas, and its brand needed to become more relevant to the new businesses and also more contemporary. The brand's value proposition might change. Schlumberger is now selling service systems rather than individual service offerings. These business-strategy changes mean that the brand strategy and execution may not provide the brand the support the new strategy requires. The brand strategy needs to be driven by and support the business strategy. It does not have the luxury of being managed independently.

BUT—how much change is really needed? Does the brand vision and execution need to start over? Or can it be adapted with minor changes or reorientation? Can the existing equity in the brand vision and its execution be modified to be the basis of a new brand direction? Can the effort simply be a turn in direction instead of a new vehicle?

Fifth, the brand and offering may lack energy and visibility, appearing tired and old-fashioned. As a result, the brand is increasingly less relevant, especially to younger buyers and those customers of competitors who are receptive to a brand change. Energy creation then needs to become a priority, and the existing brand vision and execution may not be up to the task. Chapter 16 discusses the lack of energy in brands and approaches that work to add energy.

BUT—a complete redo and relaunch of the brand may not be needed or even feasible. A relatively minor augmentation of the brand vision or its execution may create enough energy to make a difference. How basic and pervasive is the energy problem? What are the options? Is it an offering problem? If so, will any brand effort be futile? In the case of car brands that have lost relevance and need a do-over, a new model that is visibly advanced technically and functionally is usually needed. Without that proof point, no amount of brand-building programs will work.

THE POWER OF CONSISTENCY

Consistency with the brand message can be seen in most strong brands, including Coca-Cola. Coke's CMO, Joe Tripodi, attributes the success of the Coke brand to consistency over a long time period.[1] He notes that physically the logo and the package have been around for more than a century, as has the brand philosophy of positivity, optimism, and happiness. Coke sponsorships are forever. The Olympic associations date back to the 1920s and the soccer sponsorships from the 1950s. Coke has always had a place in celebrations, from a family birthday to holidays and summertime events. There are ongoing efforts to energize and contemporize the brand involving the redesign of the container, new promotions, or even the "Happiness Machine" described in Chapter 12, but the core is the same and the legacy programs continue.

Consistency wins for several reasons. First, it takes time for any brand position or brand-building program to get traction. Think of well-positioned brands like Corona beer, VISA, BMW, Whole Foods Markets, Singapore Airlines, or Muji. Their consistency over multiple decades has paid off, resulting in clear, strong brand equities and loyal customer bases. To gain a new position or reposition a current one within a short time frame is difficult what with all the clutter, no matter how clever the execution or how big the budget.

Second, a consistent brand program over time can lead to the virtual ownership of a position. It is not easy to duplicate equities that have been built over many years. Subaru dominates four-wheel drive, VISA owns scope of coverage, and Charmin means softness. Competitors are preempted and must therefore pick another route, often one that is inherently less effective. An effort by a competitor to usurp Charmin's position on the softness dimension would be difficult. Worse, the competitor's efforts to communicate softness might actually be mistaken for those of Charmin.

Third, any change has the potential to dilute what has been built up. Customers are generally not able or motivated to keep up with change and often resent something that removes the familiar. There have been open rebellions over small changes in logos, as GAP found when it had to reverse a change to a logo thought to be more contemporary.

Finally, it is cost effective. Once a strong position is created, it is difficult to dislodge and relatively easy and inexpensive to maintain because you are reinforcing instead of breaking new ground. An on-brand event or spokesperson that has been firmly associated with the brand can provide a statement that is easy to understand, remember, and link with the brand. Further, you do not have to invest in finding new positions and supporting new creative executions, a process that is expensive and uncertain.

The logic is compelling. Consistency is a key to strong brands. There needs to be a good, well-researched reason to change a brand strategy or its execution. Strategists need to make sure that the real problem is not the offering, a competitive innovation, or marketplace changes that will not be addressed with a change in brand strategy or its execution.

BEWARE OF CHANGE BIASES

Creating truly effective brand visions and executions are the goal for sure. They are the hallmark of successful brands. Given that reality, why are there so many efforts to change the branding effort even when the underlying rationale is weak? One answer is organizational biases toward change that need to be understood and countered with sound, objective analysis.

Branding professionals want to change things because change is what they are trained to do and because it is simply more fun. They are bright, creative people who are operating in a culture that emphasizes finding and solving problems, detecting and responding to trends in the market, and creating effective marketing. Doing what was done last year is "so not fun." Periodically, executives at Wells Fargo suggest removing or de-emphasizing the stagecoach symbol. Thankfully for the Wells Fargo brand, those people have always lost that argument.

Further, the way forward professionally is perceived to require showing marketing brilliance rather than implementing well a strategy developed by others. That often means a reformulated brand vision and revamped execution, perhaps with a new agency or a different event strategy. The goal is to hit pay dirt and thus enhance both professional lives and self-image.

The brand team gets overexposed to existing strategy and its execution. As result, they get bored and even irritated with the brand strategy and its execution and assume incorrectly that customers are as well. The advertising giant Rosser Reeves once claimed that if he had the second-best advertising, he would always win, because the competition would get bored and change theirs. When asked what his agency is billing the client for given they were running the same Anacin commercial over and over, he replied that it was expensive to convince the client managers not to change the advertising.

Those managing a brand are pressed to deliver market performance, and market performance is almost always inadequate. Sales growth is not up to plan and profitability is always an issue, particularly when there are return-on-asset measures in play. So the conclusion is readily reached that change is needed. Since changes in operations or offerings may be difficult, expensive, or not even feasible, brand strategy and its execution become the change candidates.

There is an aspiration trap, where a brand team engages in a futile, unsuccessful search for perfection and a dramatic improvement in performance when the probability of achieving either is actually very low. It is somewhat like the search for the fountain of youth: a compulsive and futile waste of resources. People capable of generating great ideas are rare, and the offering and market environment that allows them to thrive is rarer still. Further, when a potential winner does emerge, it needs to be proven with an expensive and risky market commitment. If the result fails to achieve a major improvement or, worse, generates a failure, a brand setback could be major.

THE BOTTOM LINE

Brand consistency can allow an effective position to build, allow a brand to own a position, make customers comfortable, and lead to cost efficiencies. A clear, compelling brand vision that endures and drives brand programs that are innovative, fresh, and contemporary should be the goal. Not all brands are so blessed, but the upside is all too clear.

Consistency does not mean strategic stubbornness about the vision or relentless repetition of a weak execution. There are very real rationales for changing a brand strategy or its execution, such as a weak or defective strategy or execution, a changing marketplace or business strategy, or a lack of energy. But a change should be justified and biases toward change should be identified and resisted. To guard against brand-change decisions that are premature or unwarranted, the case for change should be as objective and comprehensive as possible. It should not be left to someone's instinct.

Chapter 14

INTERNAL BRANDING: A KEY INGREDIENT

Culture eats strategy for breakfast.
—**Peter Drucker**

T est your organization by asking employees these two questions: What does your brand stand for? Do you care? If employees don't answer both questions positively, there is little chance that the business strategy will be implemented successfully. The goal of internal branding is to make sure that employees know the brand vision, and critically, that they actually care.

Having a strong internal brand has several benefits.

First, a clear, compelling internal brand provides direction and motivation to employees and partners. Living a brand involves a host of decisions, and brand clarity will provide guidance. People and teams will be more likely to know whether a decision or program is "on-brand." As a result, there will be a reduced tendency to risk the brand with inappropriate associations or programs.

Second, the internal brand can also inspire employees to find and implement creative, breakthrough brand-building programs—to stretch for a "big" idea. There is always the tendency to allow the prior programs and budget allocations to be the roadmap of the future. A motivated workforce that can see where the brand message or delivery is not being heard in the marketplace can create innovative programs that will make a difference.

Third, an employee base that is energized by a strong brand will be motivated to talk about the brand to others. Whether that employee is a salesman talking to a retail buyer, a consultant living with a client, a bank teller interacting with customers, an engineer at a car firm talking to his or her Twitter followers, or an appliance executive talking to a neighbor, there is a chance for an influential communication, which could even go viral. But it requires that the employee know and care about the brand.

Fourth, a brand with a vision that includes a higher purpose is likely to provide employees with meaning and even fulfillment in the job. The higher purpose could be, for example, creating "insanely" good products, improving customer's lives, or making progress toward sustainability. It can represent an energizing common goal that leads to more productive and committed employees.

Fifth, an activated internal brand strategy can support the organizational culture, which can be a foundation of a strategy and its implementation. A culture contains a set of values that underlie offerings. A brand vision often contains part or all of these values in addition to offering-focused dimensions and thus can not only support the culture but can provide a rationale for it, by linking it to the customer and business strategy.

Internal branding is always important, but there are circumstances in which it becomes vital to the success, even survival, of the enterprise, such as when a new brand vision has been created because:

- The absence of a brand vision or the conclusion that the existing one was ineffective was seen to affect the ability of the business strategy to succeed.
- There has been a merger or acquisition and two strategies, cultures, and brands need to be integrated, sometimes quickly.
- The business strategy and perhaps the senior management team have changed and the organization needs to set off on a new direction.

In each of these cases, there is an opportunity as well as a challenge. There is an opportunity to launch or relaunch the new internal brand with all the attendant attention. The challenge is to get it right and to follow through so that the brand vision will not become an empty promise.

Bringing the internal brand to life starts with two imperatives. First, there needs to be a clear and compelling brand vision that can be shown to be doable and successful in the marketplace. Second, there has to be support from the top management team. They have to believe that having a strong brand internally is vital for the success of the business strategy. If the CEO and top management are not on board, the effort will not have legs. Engaging top management by involving them in the development of the brand vision or getting them in contact with customers to realize the competitive context may need to be part of the process.

COMMUNICATING THE BRAND INTERNALLY

How do you communicate the brand to employees? To start, different employee segments defined by organizational roles and authority levels will require different programs. For example, different communication programs will be appropriate for top executives vs. those in front of customers vs. those playing an internal brand ambassador role.

For each segment, the program should reflect the fact that there are three stages that employees need to pass. The first is "learning" about the brand vision, what it entails and how it is different from other brands. The second is "believing," to accept the idea that the brand can deliver behind the vision and that the vision will lead to success. The third is "living" the brand, to be inspired and empowered to make the vision happen and to be an advocate for that vision internally and externally.

The *learning* path can and should involve all the communication vehicles available such as newsletters, workshops, and personal efforts brand ambassadors, senior managers, influencers, and others. A brand book and brand card are helpful if surrounded by the right culture. A brand book in print or video form is not a rule book with dos and don'ts with respect to fonts (although that has its own role), but an inspiring and informative communication based on visual and conceptual metaphors and stories that provide texture to the brand vision. It can be amplified by being part of an intranet site that is used during training or when making presentations. A brand card, on which the key vision elements are set forth and elaborated in a convenient form, can be powerful, especially if the CEO refers to it regularly.

The learning effort should go beyond communicating the vision. It should link the vision to the business strategy, making clear that there is a reason for the vision to live. Executives explaining in print, video, or in person the "what and why" behind the business strategy and the role of the internal brand vision, should play a key role. The learning effort can be motivated by highlighting gaps between the aspirational brand vision and the current reality. Challenges such as "the customer experience is not on-brand," "the innovation stream is not adequate," or "the higher-purpose needs programs to get traction" can be posed. If there is excessive focus on the vision itself, there is a risk of precipitating an "I disagree" position.

The *believing* stage involves a more extensive set of communication events, but the more important step is to put substance behind the brand vision to signal that the organization is committed. Two steps can make the point. First, put visible programs in place to make the brand vision and its associated business strategy actually succeed. That might mean a culture-changing training program, an offering innovation plan, an advertising program, or a customer-experience enhancement, but it will have substance and will involve investment.

A second element is to align the evaluation and reward of people and programs around the new initiative. Measurement and rewards drive behavior. At IBM during the early 1990s, when the firm was in deep financial trouble and was poised to be broken up into seven parts, Lou Gerstner entered with a brand vision to deliver integrated solutions for clients—solutions that spanned the firm. As part of the task of creating a culture of cooperation with a very siloed organization, the evaluation of people de-emphasized financial performance of silo units and added a dimension reflecting the ability of people to demonstrate cross-organization cooperation. This sent a huge signal to the firm.

The *living* stage, where people are inspired to action, is the most difficult and crucial. It needs to go beyond communication to behavior. Workshops can play an important role. Participants can be asked to:

- Build visual montages that represent the brand vision dimensions.
- Evaluate existing programs with respect to the extent they are "on-brand."
- Describe a prototypical customer in each segment in terms of their personality, vacation choice, books read, etc.
- Develop new programs to enhance the brand using creative techniques. For example, consider the "worst ideas" and how they might be altered to work. Or engage in lateral thinking by using, for example, a random object like a hammer, as a starting point.
- Ask what they will do differently in their job going forward to enhance the brand.
- Role-play interacting with customers.

Team task forces can play a role. Microsoft, for example, has the "Microsoft Green Teams" that look for ways to further their "green" initiative through outreach programs into the community or through internal communication programs. Such teams can develop and implement their own initiatives and, more important, involve key people in the vision.

Getting employees in front of customers can be one way to make the brand vision have priority. P&G, for example, puts executives in front of customers regularly in the home and in the store (with "shop-alongs" or as behind-the-counter participants). Some organizations encourage their people to regularly interact with customers via tweets or other mechanism. When an executive interacts with customers first-hand and sees more vividly the issues, the importance of creating and supporting an internal brand is more visible.

Employee engagement can come indirectly. Sometimes it is easier to get engagement for a key brand-building program. Heineken, for example, used an internal table football competition (soccer in the United States) to create enthusiasm for one of their key brand builders, the UEFA Champions League sponsorship. More than eight thousand employees participated, and 85 percent of those felt the game represented the core values of Heineken. Another firm had employees help create a huge tapestry of imagery representing the brand values, which was prominently displayed in the home office.

Organizationally, there should be a brand champion—someone or some team that is in charge of the brand and willing to carry the flag. He or she should be a primary internal brand spokesperson, communicating the brand idea to colleagues and encouraging them to find creative ways to communicate the brand to others. The brand champion should also protect the brand against misuse or going off-brand with respect to brand extensions, co-branding, promotions, sponsorships, and other programs. The brand champion might create a team of brand ambassadors—people to represent the brand throughout the organization. Individually, these people should have credibility within the organization, have initiative, and be good at involving others.

One last observation. Communicating and energizing the brand internally will be much easier if the brand vision is used as a criterion for selecting and retaining employees. In Chapter 5, Zappos.com was introduced as an organization whose exceptional service level was based on values that include delivering "wow" experiences with an out-of-the-box attitude of being weird. Zappos.com selects employees who will fit those values. One of the screening questions is to name something weird that you have done. The evaluation during the trial period also involves whether they fit the weird value and others. Another organization for which values guides hiring decisions is Harrah's. With a goal of hiring people who were exceptionally upbeat and positive, Harrah's held an "American Idol" type of audition with a set of judges who selected the finalist.

SIGNATURE STORIES

Signature stories—those that represent the brand at its core and have lived over time—can be powerful aids in bringing the brand to life in the marketplace but especially internally, where they have a natural home. Stories in general are powerful communication and information storage vehicles. They potentially can communicate both simple and complex messages in a way that is involving and memorable, and do so with authenticity.

One type of story will reflect the firm's heritage and tell a brand-value story that is authentic and powerful. In 1912, Leon Leonwood Bean, frustrated by getting wet feet when hunting, developed a boot with waterproof rubber bottoms and lightweight leather tops. The boots worked so well he offered them for sale. When the first hundred pairs that sold through the mail had a stitching problem, the L.L. Bean firm refunded the customers' money and started over, a decision that led to the legendary L.L. Bean "Guarantee of 100% Satisfaction" and heritage of quality and honesty. The Williams-Sonoma pioneers, Chuck Williams and Howard Lester, had a clear, well-articulated brand vision at the outset of what Williams-Sonoma should stand for—culinary expertise, serious cooks, functional products, best-of-category offering, style reflecting taste and flair, and innovation in entertaining. This heritage has guided the firm since.

Stories can also be based on exceptional decisions or actions by employees, or out-of-the-ordinary customer experiences that provide aspiration and emotion to the brand. The famous story of how a Nordstrom employee in Alaska took back a used tire even though Nordstrom's had never sold tires (although the Nordstrom store site had once housed a tire store) shows how Nordstrom's return policy and customer focus drive their brand. Johnson & Johnson demonstrated its priorities when it responded to a Tylenol poison scare by pulling its products from the stores and redesigning the package—clearly indicating that its reputation for trust and safety was more important than the cost of a recall.

Keeping innovation and product vitality alive internally is a key need for most firms. Stories about new products that led to major business platforms can illustrate the innovation style and drivers of the organization. Patagonia, built by mountain climbers, responded to an observation that their leading product, reusable hard-steel-pylons used to hold climbing ropes, despoiled the rock surface. As a result, they invented a replacement product, aluminum chocks, that could be wedged in and removed by hand without the use of a hammer, and thus took their business strategy and brand in a new direction. The story of how the "it floats" property of Ivory soap was "invented" by a product mistake shows that P&G can recognize new product opportunities and capitalize on them. The 3M Post-it notes concept was due to a 3M engineer who needed a bookmark that would not flutter to the floor while he sang in a choir and realized there was a role for an inferior adhesive. The 3M lesson is that when an innovation fails to meet its objective, changing the objective might result in a new productive path.

It is also helpful to have a flow of contemporary stories to keep the brand fresh. And a firm that has lost the founder, has changed strategy, or has undergone a merger may not have a heritage story. In that case, signature stories will have to be discovered or created. Further, because there are a variety of contexts for which a story is helpful, having a story data bank is worthwhile.

The experience of Mobil, now Exxon-Mobil, is instructive. In part to identify internal role models, Mobil ran a contest for its employees to identify the programs and activities that best represent the Mobil brand thrust of leadership, partnership, and trust. The winner got to go to an event sponsored by Mobil, such as the Indy 500, and receive insider status. The contest received more than three hundred entries and involved many more throughout the organization in the brand vision. A useful by-product was a set of role models that could be used to elaborate the brand vision, give it depth and emotion, and be a source for future signature stories.

A challenge is to keep the signature stories visible and alive. One way is to have a history or heritage slot on the firm's Intranet and on the brand website. Another is to represent the key stories with symbols. L.L. Bean has the giant statue of the first boot. HP has the garage in Palo Alto where Bill Hewett and David Packard started the firm, and a virtual museum where the first products, including their first oscillator, are shown. Another is to have an event or recognition linked to the story.

THE EXTERNAL AND INTERNAL BRANDS

There is relationship between external and internal branding. The two branding efforts will reinforce each other. It helps if they are coordinated, with the common elements clearly specified. Sometimes they can be identical, which makes the synergy easier to achieve.

The external brand, often with a large budget and creative communication programs, will be seen by the employees. United Airlines' "Friendly Skies" external branding effort was intended to influence the employees by making visible their brand promise and to show how customers are affected when the promise is fulfilled.

The internal brand will drive the efforts that influence the external brand. It can be more aspirational than the external brand, containing dimensions that the organization aspires to deliver but lacks the ability to do so. To deliver on an aspirational dimension, a change in culture, the development of new assets, or a modification in the offering may be required. The inclusion of aspirational elements can inspire and guide employees to actively work toward their emergence. In external brand building, such aspirational elements may need to be sidelined until the brand can deliver.

In one study involving the top five hundred firms in Sweden, those that emphasized the brand vision both internally and externally were significantly more profitable (14.4 percent) than those that used it primarily to drive the culture internally (11.3 percent), those that considered a brand primarily as a device to promote an offering externally (9.6 percent), and those that viewed a brand vision cynically (8.0 percent).[1]

THE BOTTOM LINE

Powerful brands are built from the inside out. To create a strong brand in the marketplace, employees and partners need to both know the brand vision and care about its realization. A clear, motivating internal brand will provide guidance and motivation to create programs that will move the brand forward and avoid programs that will confuse or undercut the promise. Creating a strong internal brand involves three stages—"learning it," "believing it," and "living it"—aimed at key participants such as top executives, customer-facing employees, and internal brand ambassadors. Signature stories should be gathered and leveraged to support the brand in a vivid, authentic way.

PART IV

Maintain Relevance

Chapter 15

THREE THREATS TO BRAND RELEVANCE

Little Red Riding Hood, after a path into the woods was altered by a Giant, and her companion suggested another way: "My mother warned me to never stray from the path."
Companion: "The path has strayed from you."
—**Stephen Sondheim,** *Into the Woods*

A brand should aspire to grow, to win, and even to dominate. But it should also aspire to avoid losing by becoming irrelevant. The danger facing most brands is that a substantial and growing customer segment or segments will stop considering the brand as an acceptable option.[1]

There are three ways in which a brand can lose relevance:

- The subcategory (or category) to which the brand is attached is declining or changing.
- A reason-not-to-buy has emerged.
- The brand is losing energy and visibility.

SUBCATEGORY IS DECLINING

A significant threat in dynamic markets occurs when customers are no longer buying what the brand is perceived to be making. New subcategories (or categories) are emerging as competitors' innovations create "must haves." Or new trends, such as healthy eating, stimulate some subcategories and penalize others.

If a group of customers wants hybrid sedans instead of SUVs, it simply does not matter how good an SUV people think you have. They might still respect your SUV brand, believing it has the best quality and value on the market. They may even love it and recommend it to any friend interested in an SUV. And if they ever buy another SUV, they will buy yours. But your brand will not be relevant to the hybrid sedan buyer who has moved on. That may be true even if your brand also makes hybrid sedans, because the brand might lack visibility or credibility in the hybrid arena.

Losing relevance in this way is insidious in part because it can happen gradually. Further, it can happen even if the brand is strong, the customers are loyal, and the offering, benefiting from incremental innovations, has never been better. The irony is that a source of brand strength can become a relevance liability when the marketplace changes. Recall the analysis of the Japanese beer market from Chapter 7, in which Asahi in 1986 introduced Asahi Super Dry and took more than ten share points away from Kirin Lager in a short time after Kirin, the king of lager beers in Japan, had enjoyed a 60 percent share for some twenty-five years. Kirin's lager reputation made it impossible to counter the change with a Kirin Dry beer; the Kirin brand simply lacked credibility.

The ultimate tragedy is to achieve brilliance in creating differentiation, winning the "my brand is better than your brand" preference battle, and creating brand energy and visibility only to have that effort wasted because of a relevance problem. Consider a pay telephone company that has controlled the very best locations or a newspaper with the best editorial staff. Making the assumption that brand weakness is a brand-preference issue can lead to wasteful off-target initiatives that do not address what is really going on.

There are five response strategies available to a brand that is or might soon be at risk of losing subcategory relevance because what the customer is buying is changing.

Gain Parity

The goal is to create an option to a competitor's "must have" that is close enough in performance so that the brand is no longer excluded. McDonald's, facing a threat from Starbucks to their breakfast and snack dayparts, introduced the McCafe line that created for many customers a point of parity with Starbucks with respect to coffee quality, close enough to escape being an excluded option.

One challenge facing the parity option is that the brand may be perceived as lacking credibility in the new arena. Another is that it might be difficult to actually deliver on a parity option given the fact that the culture, assets, and skills of the firm were not designed to support the parity initiative.

Leapfrog the Innovation.

Instead of being satisfied with having a parity product, a firm could attempt to take over the new category or subcategory, or at least to become a significant player with a substantial or transformational innovation, leapfrogging the competitor. Nike, with its Nike + shoes and iPod Sensor, allows a runner to hear music plus keep a record of each workout. The Adidas miCoach leapfrogs Nike with features such as the Coach Circle (links you with a trainer), the SMART RUN (a trainer on your wrist), and the Support Discussions (to get answers to workout questions). Cisco many times faced a gap in their product line that they filled with an acquisition. They then added Cisco-driven synergy and systems benefits, creating a leapfrog result.

The leapfrog strategy often requires a substantial or transformational innovation, not easily accomplished. Further, getting established in a marketplace in which a competitor likely has scale and momentum will be difficult, even for an impressive innovation.

Reposition

Modify and reposition the brand so that its value proposition becomes more relevant given the market dynamics. L.L. Bean, built on a heritage of hunting, fishing, and camping, repositioned to a broader outdoor firm relevant to the interests of outdoor enthusiasts such as hikers, mountain bikers, cross-country skiers, and water-sports enthusiasts. The outdoors was still treated with the same sense of awe, respect, and adventure, but from a different perspective.

The challenge is to have enough substance to earn credibility in the new position and to implement the rebranding strategy as well. L.L. Bean had to live the new position and provide benefits that were relevant.

Stick to Your Knitting

Rather than adapting, keep pursuing the same strategy with the same value proposition, but just do it better. As noted in Chapter 13, the safety razor was threatened in the 1930s with the electric shaver and its compelling benefits. However, an incredible stream of innovations from Gillette allowed it to beat back the new category and enjoy robust growth. In-N-Out Burger, a chain in the western United States that has developed intense loyalty with a menu of burgers, fries, and shakes, has made no effort to adjust to the healthy trend. They simply continue to deliver the same menu with uncompromising quality, consistency, and service under the assumption that a worthwhile segment has ignored the healthy trend and another will indulge periodically.

The risk is that the new category or subcategory might be based on such a strong trend or such a compelling set of benefits that avoiding it might prove futile, even disastrous.

Disinvest or Exit

If none of the first four response strategies is attractive or even feasible, the remaining alternative is to disinvest—to withhold or withdraw resources from the business or to exit. This strategy involves shifting investments from a declining product market to one that is rising. Procter & Gamble has exited from most of its food businesses, for example, and invested in cosmetics and skin care, for which the growth and margins are better. GE has gone into a host of renewable energy businesses, invested in the medical arena, and disinvested or exited from more mature industries. The act of disinvesting or exiting from a business is a very painful but vital part of a firm's ability to deal with dynamic markets.

The risk of the disinvestment decision is that the trend could slow, stabilize, or even reverse itself, and the market could again become attractive when the brand has lost the capacity to be a player. Projecting the future is not easy. In late 1960s, there were dozens of articles and reports detailing why the "checkless society" was just around the corner, and firms needed to adjust to that "fact." But check-writing actually increased during the following two decades, flatten out only in the early 1990s, and it was not until around 2004 that it started to decline sharply. Even in 2010 it was still higher than credit card transactions. As Yogi Berra said, "The future ain't what it used to be."

Select the Right Response

The selection of the optimal response will be context-specific, but it will involve two difficult questions: What is the size of the relevance threat and its supporting trend? And what is a realistic judgment about the firm's ability to engage in gaining parity, leapfrogging, or repositioning? Does it have the ability to innovate, add needed capabilities, and be successful in the marketplace?

A BRAND NEGATIVE HAS BECOME A "REASON NOT TO BUY"

A loss of relevance can also occur when a brand negative, such as a quality issue or an action, policy, or program that was disliked by a substantial segment, becomes a "reason not to buy." Perrier once faced a water-contamination problem that struck at the very basis of their brand equity and negatively affected their distribution and image. Some avoid Nike because they perceive that Nike factories exploit foreign workers. A boycott of Nestle, over a perceived over-promotion of infant formula as a substitute for breast milk because it could lead to the distress and even death of babies of the poor who lack access to unpolluted water, has gone on for more than three decades. Even minor product characteristics can matter. Some customers, for example, would not buy some German car brands because they did not have cup holders.

There are two general approaches to dealing with "reason not to buy" relevance: 1) negating the negatives by addressing them head-on, and 2) changing the discussion.

Negate the Negative

At the turn of the twenty-first century in the U.S. market, Hyundai was fighting the perception that Korean cars were of poor quality and that their brand was boring. As a result, Hyundai faced two sets of "reasons not to buy."

Programs initiated in 1998 created cars designed and manufactured to deliver high quality, and by 2004 the brand had gone from near the bottom of the J.D. Powers Initial Quality Study to near the top. Despite the change in actual quality, the perception lingered until Hyundai put in place a compelling quality-change story. An aggressive warranty branded as the Hyundai Advantage, the industry's first ten-year, 100,000-mile warranty on the power train, was marketed as "America's Best Warranty." The Advantage told the quality story in graphic terms—and gained enormous visibility. The brand's quality image got a huge boost when the Hyundai Genesis, a Lexus-level car, was introduced and won the 2009 Car of the Year award at the Detroit Auto Show. Well-executed advertising on the Super Bowl, the World Cup, and other prestige events supported.

The "boring" stigma was based on being a me-too follower and having uninspiring designs that lacked distinctiveness. Two programs countered that image. One was the Hyundai Assurance program, whereby during the financial crash of 2008 Hyundai pledged to buy back any car if a customer lost a job. This program was regarded as a creative and empathetic response to the economic uncertainly facing the United States. Another was a visible design approach branded as "Fluidic Sculpture," which produced cars with designs so appealing that Hyundai car design changed from a liability to an asset.

By removing negatives, Hyundai moved from nowhere to capturing 5 percent or so of the U.S. car market. Perhaps just as amazing, its relevance level increased to the point that around 30 percent of the car-buying public said they would consider Hyundai.

Change the Discussion

Attacking a negative directly, to prove it no longer exists or never did, is tempting. However, such an effort can serve to remind people about the problem and the firm's lack of credibility around it. It can be more effective to change the conversation, to provide another perspective so that the negatives will not automatically be top-of-mind and the center of discussion.

In 2005, Walmart was boycotted by 8 percent of the population and had an unfavorable image among others. These segments were disturbed by Walmart's perceived ill-treatment of employees and suppliers, its huge program to buy from China suppliers, and its perceived effort to destroy small retailers. Walmart learned that efforts to deal with these issues head-on only tended to make them worse by raising their visibility. An effort to change the conversation was more successful.

It all started on a camping trip in 2004, when the chairman, Rob Walton, was challenged to become a leader in environmental programs. The result was a major corporate sustainability initiative involving employees, trucks, stores, warehouses, suppliers, communities, and customers. Fourteen teams—consisting of Walmart executives, suppliers, environmental groups, and regulators—were formed to focus on sustainability in areas such as store operations, logistics, packaging, and use of forest products. Suppliers of environmentally responsive products or packaging, from salmon fishermen in Alaska to Unilever (whose compact detergent uses less space and packaging material than other similar products), were not only favored but supported.

The result was energy reductions that had national significance and a surprisingly sharp reduction in costs. Further, it turned out that the increased presence of organic food and even clothes made from organic cotton in the stores was valued by customers. A program that started out with a motivation to do the right thing ended up to be a very profitable investment.

Important to the relevance issue, the program caused the brand to soar on the social responsibility dimension, driven in part by the story behind the program and in part on the results, both of which got significant attention.[2] Perceptions of Walmart may have been summarized best by an article headlined "It's Hard to Hate Walmart Anymore."[3] The dialogue around the Walmart brand was affected. There was an alternative to focusing on the negatives. The relevance challenge was not over for Walmart, but it was greatly alleviated, and the trajectory was positive—a remarkable change, given where the firm had stood only a few years before.

Playing Defense Can Work

The tendency for all managers is to try to improve the offering—to add positives. It may be more productive to address negatives, to make the brand relevant to a larger group. But it is not enough simply to address the negatives functionally; there must be a way to credibly communicate to a group that may have put the brand in the graveyard (familiar brands that are "out of mind" at purchase decision time), a place where communication does not get through. The story needs to be told, and in that effort a brand like Fluidic Sculpture or a visible program like the Walmart environmental initiative can help.

BRAND HAS LOST ENERGY

A loss of brand energy is the third threat to brand relevance. Energy is crucial to relevance because energy creates visibility, and being relevant requires that the brand come to mind at the right time. A brand that loses energy and thus visibility will be lost in the clutter and noise of the environment, and will no longer be relevant. A brand without energy might also be considered tired, old-fashioned, and bland, and thus no longer acceptable.

The next chapter will discuss three approaches to injecting energy into a brand—creating new offering vitality, energizing marketing programs, or finding or developing a branded energizer to which a target brand can link.

THE BOTTOM LINE

It is a great feeling to win, but it can be equally productive to avoid losing relevance among an important part of the marketplace. Maintaining relevance is usually easier and more cost effective than relying on big wins and it can set the stage for future winning strategies.

A brand can lose relevance in any of three ways. A declining subcategory can be addressed by gaining parity along a deficient dimension, leapfrogging to superiority, repositioning your brand, applying the stick-to-your-knitting strategy, disinvesting, or exiting. A "reason-not-to-buy" can be neutralized by "negating the negative," or by changing the discussion. The third threat is a loss of energy which will be discussed in the next chapter.

The challenge is to be aware of and sensitive to these relevance threats. They can be addressed, but only if they are identified and understood. Like attacking a serious illness, the earlier you can detect an emerging relevance issue, the easier it will be to create an effective response. Detection is not always easy. It requires a market research capability, the ability to get insights from data, and people who are strategically sensitive to marketplace changes and emerging brand weaknesses.

Chapter 16

ENERGIZE YOUR BRAND!

*A relationship, I think, is like a shark. It has to
constantly move forward or it dies. And I think
what we've got on our hands is a dead shark.*
—**Woody Allen,** *Annie Hall*

U nless your brand is one of the exceptions, it needs energy! It
needs to have at least one of the following characteristics:

- **Interesting/Exciting**. There is a reason to talk about the brand.
  (examples: AXE, NASCAR, Pixar, Red Bull, FedEx Cup.)
- **Involving/Engaging**. People are engaged with the brand; it
  can be part of a valued activity or lifestyle. (examples: LEGO,
  Disney, Starbucks, Google, Amazon.)
- **Innovative/Dynamic**. The brand has been capable of creating
  "must have" innovations that define new subcategories or has had
  a flow of incremental but visible innovations. (examples: Apple,
  Virgin, GE, 3M.)

- **Passionate/Purpose-Driven**. The brand conveys a higher purpose that propels passion. (examples: Whole Foods Market, Patagonia, MUJI, Method, Ben & Jerry's, Kashi.)

A brand that has insufficient energy has three potential liabilities. First, it will lack visibility and thus be less likely to be considered, a necessary condition to be relevant. Second, a loss of energy can lead to the brand being perceived as bland, tired, old-fashioned, and not up-to-date. The brand no longer fits a customer's self-image or lifestyle, has negative self-expressive and social benefits, and is so yesterday. Third, a loss of brand energy can result in declines in key image elements. The reality of these declines is backed up by disturbing evidence.

The Y&R Brand Asset Valuator (BAV) database includes forty thousand brands measured on over seventy-five metrics in more than forty countries, from 1993 to today. The book *The Brand Bubble,* by John Gerzema and Ed Lebar, reports findings from the BAV database that brand equities, as measured by trustworthiness, esteem, perceived quality, and awareness, have been falling sharply over the years.[1] For example, in a ten- to twelve-year period starting in the mid-1990s, trustworthiness dropped nearly 50 percent; esteem fell by 12 percent; brand quality perceptions fell by 24 percent; and, remarkably, even awareness fell by 24 percent. This fall has continued since that analysis, even accelerated.

The exceptions to this decline are those brands with energy. They have, in general, not only resisted an image decline but have retained their ability to drive financial performance. An increase in brand energy has been shown to increase both usage and preference. In addition, a BAV modeling effort by Bob Jacobson of Washington and Natalie Mizik of Columbia shows that for high-energy brands, increases in energy and attitude drive stock return (based on an analysis of those brands like GE or IBM that represent a significant part of the sales of a firm).[2] In fact, the BAV team has redefined differentiation, now calling it "energized differentiation" because without energy, the impact of differentiation is compromised.

How can you energize a brand? There are three routes that every brand should explore: provide new offering vitality, energize marketing, and find or create a branded energizer.

NEW OFFERING VITALITY

One way to maintain brand energy is through offering innovation. Dove, GE, Samsung, Columbia Sportswear, and others have a continuous flow of offering innovations that create interest, visibility, and energy.

Adding or enhancing energy to healthy brands is one challenge. A bigger one is to reenergize brands that are tired and have seen their energy fade. In those circumstances, a meaningful product or service innovation can play a critical role. When the brand is in a category for which customers receive self-expressive and social benefits, a significant offering innovation that can credibly make the statement that the brand is now different can be an imperative. Without such a statement offering, no amount of claims of change will work.

Cadillac revitalized its brand behind quality improvements and marketing, but a crucial ingredient was a new award-winning car, the CTS. The car was not a stand-alone innovation, but was linked to the historical prestige of the brand, which had been allowed to drift into irrelevance. Leveraging a brand's heritage, while still finding ways to contemporize it, can be the key element in brand revitalization. The fact is that, however difficult, it is usually easier to revitalize a tired brand than to create a new one. In the case of Cadillac, however, the revitalization would not have succeeded without the tangible proof point of a new model.

ENERGIZE MARKETING

Creating a visible, impactful offering innovation may be a rare occurrence for most brands. Further, in some product categories, take hot dogs or insurance, for example, which are either mature, boring, or both, new product vitality is not a practical energy source. Thus, there are many contexts in which creating dramatic marketing programs becomes an alternative and more accessible route to brand energy than generating offering innovations. Some illustrative programs follow.

- **An involving promotion.** Denny's gave away more than two million Grand Slam Breakfasts in one day with the help of a Super Bowl commercial and online buzz. The offer of free breakfasts broke through the noise.

- **Compelling advertising**. Old Spice features Isaiah Mustafa— former NFL star, actor, and possessor of a cut body—telling women he's "the man your man could smell like." The original ad garnered 44 million online views in two years; it energized Old Spice and propelled it to a leadership position over sporty Right Guard and sexy AXE.
- **Go retail**. The Apple store is a good part of the success of its products and brand because it has energy and is so on-brand. Nike, Panasonic, and Sony also have statement stores that serve to present their brand and product story in a compelling and integrative way.
- **A higher-order purpose**. A "higher purpose" can energize employees and customers, as was explained in Chapter 5, using cases such as Crayola's goal of helping parents and teachers to raise inspired, creative children; Apple's aspiration to build insanely great products; and Patagonia's "reduce, repair, reuse, and recycle" customer action program.
- **A viral video**. As described in Chapter 12, DC Shoes used a stunt driver to create videos that went viral and Coke enhanced its energy with the "Happiness Machine" video.

Of the four dimensions of brand energy, the one that is both the most accessible and powerful for many brands is the Involving/ Engaging dimension, activated by programs like a go-to website with an active community. The key to winning on this dimension, as noted in Chapter 11, is to focus on the customer's sweet spot—interests and activities that are an important part of their identity, values, and lifestyle. Think of the mayoclinic.com online site, where more than three thousand physicians and scientists from the Mayo Clinic share current medical information about diseases, symptoms, drugs, supplements, tests, and general health. Or the Nature Valley Trail View site, where the great trails in four national parks can be viewed from the perspective of the hiker.

FIND OR CREATE A BRANDED ENERGIZER

A third brand energy-creating option is to develop or find a branded energizer, something with energy, and attach your brand to it. There are two types—the ownable internal branded energizer and the external brand energizer.

Ownable, Internal Branded Energizer

An ownable, internal branded energizer is a branded product, promotion, sponsorship, symbol, program, or other entity that by association significantly enhances and energizes a target brand and is developed and owned by the organization.

Several examples of branded energizers are motivated by customer sweet spots and were introduced in Chapter 11. One was the Oscar Mayer Wienermoble, the eight hot dog-shaped vehicles that visit kid's events and support the Oscar Mayer jingle contest. Another was the Avon Walk for Breast Cancer, which provides energy to the cosmetics firm that could not be obtained through the offering. Still others were the involving websites such as the Pampers Village or BeautyTalk.

An internal branded energizer can be a symbol or a person. Symbols like the AFLAC duck, Betty Crocker, and the Michelin man provide enormous visibility while highlighting relevant attributes. Virgin's founder and CEO, Richard Branson, with his outlandish stunts (some involving hot-air balloons) have become a large part of the energy and personality of the Virgin brand.

External Branded Energizer

Creating and owning an internal branded energizer that resonates with the target segments and will energize and enhance the target brand is difficult and expensive. It can take years to get traction at a time in which action may be needed in months. Indeed, it may not be feasible at all in a marketplace in which competitors have strong brands and active energizers of their own. An alternative is an "external branded energizer," a brand that is owned by another organization. In essence, you find a brand already established with energy and attach the target brand to it.

There is practically an infinite supply of brands outside the organization that have the potential to energize and enhance that also have enormous strength, are not tied to competitors, and can be linked to the target brand. With discipline and creativity candidates can be located. The challenge then is to create and manage the resulting co-brand alliance. An external branded energizer will have a variety of sources, but among the most important are sponsorships and endorsements.

The right sponsorship, handled well, can energize and even transform a brand, adding a meaningful higher purpose. Home Depot, for example, sponsors Habitat for Humanity, as was described in Chapter 11. FedEx has gotten energy by sponsoring the FedEx Cup, the world series of professional golf that culminates in four tournaments, the last of which contains only thirty top golfers vying for a $10 million top prize. The venerable motor oil brand Valvoline gains involvement and a visible shared interest through its NASCAR sponsorship, supported by a creative, involving website.

Another route is using an endorser—a personality that is contemporary, visible, on-brand, energetic, authentic, and in the news. Think of what LeBron James brings to not only Nike but to Coca-Cola, Samsung, State Farm, and McDonalds. An endorser can also be a symbol, like the Charlie Brown characters adapted by MetLife in 1985 or the Pink Panther used by Owens Corning, the insulation company, even earlier. These symbols can provide energy and visibility to a brand stuck in a boring product class.

Some Branded Energizer Guidelines

A branded energizer will have a better chance for success if it has these attributes:

- **Has energy itself.** An energizer brand needs to have its own energy. However good the fit and clever the execution, if the energizer lacks its own energy, the investment will be wasted. Further, the energizer's energy should not be transitory but should be expected to increase or at least retain its energy over time.
- **Creates an emotional connection.** An emotional connection with customers and potential customers communicates much more about a brand than does a set of facts and logic and enhances the relationship as well. The emotional message is punchier and simpler. Pedigree's Adoption Drive, with its pictures of adorable dogs, triggers an emotional response and gives the Pedigree brand a life as something more than just a firm that makes pet food.

- **Is authentic**. The program should not feel contrived or commercial. If the brand has a logical fit and the program's objective is program-oriented, a feeling of authenticity will be more likely to prevail. Crest's Healthy Smiles, for example, which provides low-cost dental care for poor children, has a clear fit with Crest. Authenticity comes easier when the organization can be part of the program by leveraging its people, resources, and competencies—as Home Depot does with their Habitat for Humanity connection—rather than being simply a detached sponsor.
- **Connects to the master brand**. The branded energizer cannot play its role of providing energy to the master brand unless it is connected. There are three connection routes. One is to have the name of the master brand as part of the energizer brand name, such as the Ronald McDonald House. A second is to select a program or activity that is so on-brand that it makes the link easier to establish. A water conversation program is a natural for brands like Starbucks and Coca-Cola. A third is to simply forge the link by consistently building it over time with significant link-building resources, a route that is much more costly and difficult because people are not motivated to internalize the link.
- **Is regarded as a long-term asset**. A branded energizer should be considered a long-term asset and merit a long-term investment and ongoing active management. It should have an active life of its own and not just be something on the shelf. Consider again the Avon Walk, the Oscar Mayer Wienermobile, and the Aflac duck. These energizers all have had decades of life and have themselves been continuously refreshed.
- **Is managed as part of the brand portfolio**. As long-term brand assets, branded energizers, whether internal or external, are part of the brand portfolio, with defined roles and links to the rest of the portfolio brands. They are not just ad hoc, stand-alone brands. These roles and links need to be managed as well, particularly the link between the energizer and the parent brand.

THE BOTTOM LINE

Brands with enough energy are a small minority, and those with too much energy are rare. The lack of energy is an epidemic in the brand space. Creating brand energy should be a priority for nearly every brand; inadequate energy means a reduced chance of being visible when purchases are being made, a perception of being old and boring and not-for-me, and a deterioration of the brand image. The good news is that energy can be added to a brand through new offering vitality, energized marketing programs, and finding or creating an ownable or external branded energizer.

PART V

Manage Your Brand Portfolio

Chapter 17

YOU NEED A BRAND PORTFOLIO STRATEGY

The whole is greater than the sum of its parts.
—**Aristotle**

A true story. A software firm had such a confusing set of brands and offerings that their own employees could not tell customers what they should buy. Further, new product naming was paralyzed; every naming option seemed only to make the confusion worse. Portfolio issues seldom reach such a crisis stage, but they too often inhibit business strategy and create inefficient and ineffective brand-building efforts.

All firms have multiple brands; some have hundreds, even thousands. The core problem is that each of these brands is too often managed as a stand-alone silo. Instead, the brand portfolio needs to be actively managed so that it results in:[1]

- **Clarity** instead of confusion, both internally and in the marketplace.
- **Synergy** whereby the various brands and their brand-building programs work together to enhance the visibility of the brands,

create and reinforce associations with consistency, and obtain cost efficiencies.

- **Relevance** so that brands will be in place that will provide visibility and credibility for offerings in existing and target product markets.
- **Strong brand platforms** that will be the basis of a healthy business going forward.
- **Leveraged brand assets** that are extended into new product markets as endorsers or master brands.
- **Clear brand roles**.

Creating effective brand-portfolio strategies is always extremely challenging. Multiple brands often are involved in individual offerings, like GM's Cadillac Escalade with Stabilitrak and OnStar. And each of these five offering-defining brands is linked to other GM models in often complex and subtle ways. What makes it particularly difficult is that each firm and portfolio is unique, so while there are a set of tools and concepts that are helpful, there is no linear process that will work across contexts. In addition, because the brand-portfolio strategy is driven by a business strategy that is dynamic, there is an ongoing necessity to modify, augment, and change the portfolio and its strategy. Not easy at all.

There are two portfolio decisions that should be clearly understood, not only because they will influence the portfolio's ability to achieve its objectives, but because they define and illustrate brand roles that are central to a portfolio strategy.

- First, how should a new (or existing) offering be branded? Should subbrands or endorsed brands play a role?
- Second, what are the brand priorities within the portfolio? Which brands are strategic and which should be eliminated or receive reduced support?

BRANDING A NEW OFFERING— THE BRAND RELATIONSHIP SPECTRUM

An offering needs to be represented by a customer-facing brand or set of brands, each with a defined role. These roles are key building blocks of a portfolio strategy. They include:

- **Master brand**—the primary indicator of the offering, the point of reference. Visually, it will usually take top billing.
- **Endorser brand**—serves to provide credibility and substance to the offering (e.g., Lancôme endorses product brands like Miracle). In most cases, its role is to represent the strategy, people, resources, values, and heritage of an organization behind the offering.
- **Subbrand**—augments or modifies the associations of a master brand in a specific product-market context (e.g., Porsche Carrera). Its role is to add associations such as product attributes (e.g., Chevrolet Volt), a brand personality (e.g., Calloway Big Bertha), a product category (e.g., Ocean Spray Craisins), and even energy (e.g., Nike Force).
- **Descriptors**—describe the offering, usually in functional terms (e.g., GE Aviation, GE Appliances, GE Capital, GE Healthcare). Although usually not a brand, descriptors play key roles in any portfolio strategy.

Driver Roles

The driver role reflects the degree to which a brand drives the purchase decision and defines the use experience. When a person is asked, "What brand did you buy (or use)?" the answer given will be the brand that had primary driver role. So if users of Jeep Wrangler will tend to say they bought or drove a Jeep, rather than a Wrangler, the subbrand, Wrangler, would be relegated to a minor driver role. While master brands usually have the dominant driver role; subbrands, endorsers, and branded differentiators can also play driver roles with different levels of intensity. Understanding the driver role is important in developing an offering brand or brands and subsequently managing that brand or brand set.

The Brand Relationship Spectrum

A key portfolio-strategy issue is how to brand an acquired or internally developed new offering or to rebrand an existing offering. There are four options positioned along a brand relationship spectrum as shown in Figure 6:

New brand. The most independent option is to have a new brand, unconstrained by any master brand associations that could be unhelpful or even harmful. When a collection of new brands is assembled, we have what is termed the house-of-brands strategy, meaning each brand needs its own house. P&G, a house-of-brands firm, operates more than eighty major brands with little link to P&G or to each other.

The house-of-brands strategy allows firms to position brands clearly on functional benefits and to dominate niche segments. Compromises don't have to be made in the positioning of the brand to accommodate its use in other product-market contexts. The brand connects directly to the niche customer with a targeted value proposition. In the shampoo category, for example, P&G has several brands such as Head & Shoulders (dandruff fighter), Pantene (makes hair shine), Pert Plus (the first product to combine shampoo and conditioner), Herbal Essences (nature inspired), and Wella Allure (professional quality), each of which has a unique value proposition.

BRAND ROLE	MASTER BRAND WITH DESCRIPTOR	MASTER BRAND WITH SUBBRAND	NEW BRAND ENDORSED BY MASTER BRAND	NEW BRAND
Distance from master Brand	None	Some	More	Maximum

Brand Relationship Spectrum
Figure 6

A major limitation of P&G's house-of-brands strategy is the loss of economies of scale that comes with leveraging a brand across multiple businesses. Those brands that cannot support investment themselves (especially the third or fourth P&G entry in a category) risk stagnation and decline. Another limitation is the loss of brand leverage, because focused brands tend to have a narrow range and their ability to be extended is limited.

Endorsed brand. The second option is the endorsed-brand strategy, where the offering brand, such as Scotchguard, is endorsed by an existing master brand, such as 3M. The role of the endorser brand is to provide credibility and reassurance that the endorsed brand will live up to its claims. An endorsed brand (Scotchguard) is not completely independent of the endorser (3M), but it has considerable freedom to develop product associations and a brand personality that is different from that of the endorser. The endorser brand usually has only a minor driver role, but when the endorser is strong and the new offering is unknown and risky, its driver role can become significant.

There are times in which the endorser can benefit. For example, a successful new product with energy or an offering that becomes a market leader brand can enhance an endorser. Thus, when Nestle bought Kit-Kat, a leading chocolate brand in the UK, a strong Nestle endorsement was added in order to enhance Nestlé's image in the UK.

Subbrand. The third option is the subbrand strategy, such as Wells Fargo Way2Save program or the Buick Enclave. The subbrand adds to or modifies the associations of the master brand. It could have a different personality or value proposition than the master brand, but does not have as much latitude as an endorsed brand.

A subbrand can stretch the master brand, allowing it to compete in arenas in which it otherwise would not fit. For example, the subbrand Black Crown allows Budweiser to enter the premium lager subcategory, the subbrand Evolution Kit provides Samsung with a vehicle to create a way for viewers to interact with their TV sets, and the subbrand Venus helps Gillette become relevant for women.

An important element in managing the subbrand is to understand its driver role. If it is significant, than it could merit some brand-building resources. But if it is minor and mainly plays a descriptive role, that would not be the case. The role of a subbrand is frequently exaggerated, and organizations can be shocked when research shows that the driver role if a subbrand is minimal and investments in building it have been wasted.

The Master brand. The final option, to market the new offering under an existing master brand with a descriptor, termed a branded-house option, means that the master brand will be in a dominant driver role. Any descriptor used has a very modest or nonexistent driver role. BMW has a master brand strategy with models denoted as BMW 3, BMW 7, BMW X1, BMW M, and so on. FedEx is another, with FedEx Express, FedEx Services, FedEx Freight, and more. The branded-house option maximally leverages an established master brand, requires a minimum investment in each new offering, and potentially enhances the clarity and synergy of the portfolio. As a result, it is the default option. Any other strategy requires compelling reasons.

There are two major drawbacks to the master brand strategy. First, when it adapts to different product markets, the use of same master brand without a subbrand or endorsed brand to create or modify a value proposition means that the brand may not resonate with the customers and thus could be at a competitive disadvantage. Second, it also runs the risk that a negative event or publicity in one context could harm the brand.

Hybrid strategies. There are actually few pure strategies; most are hybrids. Kraft, for example, is used as a master brand for cheese, mayonnaise, and salad dressing, but is also used as an endorser of brands like Stovetop Stuffing, Miracle Whip, Oscar Mayer, and Maxwell House, among others. L'Oreal has a set of master brands including Maybelline New York, L'Oreal Paris, and Garnier, but each of these has subbrands, and branded ingredients. Even BMW has the M (all-wheel performance) and Z4 (sports car) that play subbrand roles, with personality and other associations distinct from BMW.

Selecting the Right Position on the Spectrum

The choice of the right brand for a new offering really rests on the analysis of three questions.

- Will the existing master brand enhance the offering?
- Will the offering enhance the master brand?
- Is there a compelling reason to generate a new brand, whether it be a stand-alone brand, an endorsed brand, or a subbrand?

The optimal situation is when the master brand both enhances and benefits from being part of the new offering. When that fails to materialize, distance between the master brand and the new offering may be sought. Some distance will be created with a subbrand, more with an endorsed brand, and the most with a new brand.

It should be noted that if there is a compelling business strategy at stake, some brand risks might be necessary. We should not be under the illusion that the goal is to create and protect brands. Rather, the goal should be to create and leverage a brand portfolio to enable the business strategy to succeed.

BRAND PRIORITIES WITHIN THE PORTFOLIO

In addition to the offering-defining roles, there are a set of portfolio roles that have priority and resource allocation implications. The assignment of strategic brand status is the most critical.

A strategic brand is one with strategic importance to the organization. It is a brand that needs to become and stay strong and therefore should receive whatever resources are needed. The identification of strategic brands is a huge step toward insuring that brand-building resources are allocated to the strategically most important business arenas.

There are in general three types of strategic brands. They are brands that are:

- **Current power brands.** Currently generating significant sales and profits and not a candidate for cash cow status. Perhaps it is already a large, dominant brand, such as Microsoft Windows or Coke Zero, and is projected to maintain or grow its position.
- **Future power brands.** Projected to generate significant sales and profit in the future, such as Coca-Cola's glacéau vitaminwater. Future power brands may also be small or even yet to be introduced but earn status because of their potential and place in the portfolio of the future.
- **Linchpin brands.** Will indirectly influence (as opposed to generate) significant sales and market position in the future. These brands are the linchpin or leverage point of a major business area or of a future vision of the firm and are likely to be branded differentiators as described in Chapter 8. Hilton Rewards is such a brand for Hilton Hotels because it represents the future ability to control a substantial and critical segment in the hotel industry—those travelers involved in loyalty programs.

In addition to strategic brands, there are brand roles with resource-allocation implications, including:

- **Niche brands.** Have become dominant in a profitable niche market but will not become power brands.
- **Flanker brands.** Designed to neutralize a competitor. For example, a premium brand might introduce a value brand to thwart

a low-priced value competitor. It may not reach profitability standards, but it could be useful in reducing the market power of a competitor.

• **Cash cow brands**. Have a worthwhile business based on a core segment but have little growth potential. They should be assigned little or no investment but simply create a cash flow that can be used for other brands

The classic problem is that future power brands and lynchpin brands that have little or no sales base get starved of resources. The current power brands have both the budget and the organizational power. Often there is no organizational mechanism to take a total portfolio view; thus, the current power brands get over-investment and the brands of the future get starved. There is also the danger of wishful thinking from optimistic brand managers that will result in an excessive number of strategic brand nominees; some will receive resources that would be better spent elsewhere.

Trimming the Portfolio—An Evaluation and Consolidation Process

There is another problem—too many brands in the portfolio without clear roles. Many firms "discover" that they are over-branded, the consequence of which can range from inefficiency and confusion to paralysis in introducing new offerings and even in managing the portfolio. The prime culprit is usually a process in creating new brands that lacks discipline; there is no person or group with authority to approve or say no to the introduction of new or acquired brands and subbrands, based on an objective appraisal of whether a another brand is really warranted and will justify ongoing support.

Trimming and clarifying the portfolio is the goal of a portfolio evaluation and consolidation process—an objective analysis of the strength and utility of the existing brands and the roles they are playing in the portfolio done by a credible group of executives. In addition to pruning an over-branded portfolio, the process can identify and protect strategic brands, particularly future power and linchpin brands. It works by making the political costs of tough decisions, often with turf issues, become manageable.

The first step is to determine the relevant brand set to appraise. The brand set can include all brands and subbrands, but usually will focus on a grouping of comparable brands. For example, an analysis for GM could include its major nameplates, namely Chevrolet, Buick, Cadillac, GMC, and Opel. Another analysis level could be subbrands attached to a master brand. Thus, for Buick the subbrands would be Verano, Regal, Lacrosse, Encore, and Enclave. When brands share similar roles, it becomes easier to evaluate their relative strength.

The second step is to evaluate each brand using criteria such as its standing with respect to:

- **Brand Equity**—What is the level of awareness, perceived quality, differentiation, and relevance? Does it add or subtract value to new offerings? Oldsmobile was killed by GM in part because new models were evaluated lower when the Oldsmobile logo was added. What is the size and intensity of the loyal segment? What is the brand's driver role? Is it really just a descriptor, with little brand equity?
- **Business Strength**—What is the sales level, growth prospects, market position, and profitability of the business the brand supports? Is there enough scale to compete? Is it a market leader in its niche or is it a third- or fourth-place brand?
- **Strategic Fit**—Does it fit with the firm-wide strategic vision? Does it have the potential to extend into other categories? Can it be a growth platform or drive a market position?
- **Branding Options**—Can the brand equity be transferred to another brand? Or could it merge with other brands?

The third step is to assess the investment level for each brand based on the evaluation. The top tier will include the strategic brands. For Nestle that includes twelve global brands such as Nescafé for coffee, Nestea for tea, and Purina for pet food, plus a set of regional or country brands, such as Dreyer's Ice Cream, that are strategic in their own markets. These brands will each have a strategic role and be assigned a brand champion that can control the use of the brand and the marketing programs that affect the brand. The champion will be empowered to take a long-term strategic perspective.

Those brands that are assigned specialty roles such as being a niche brand or a flanker make up the second tier. The third tier includes those brands assigned cash cow status and given only enough investment to sustain a position, or even just enough investment to manage an orderly decline. In either case, they can generate funds to be used elsewhere.

The remaining brands will be candidates for elimination. If the underlying business is unattractive or does not fit, the brand could be sold or shut down. If the business is worthwhile but the brand is not contributing, there are two options for the brand. First, it could become a descriptor with the realization that it is not playing and will not play a driver role and receive resources. In fact, the name could be changed to a descriptor. Dell changed a host of brand names such as "E-Support" and "Ask Dudley!" to "Expert Services" and "Online Instant Answers." Second, the brand could be merged with others or have its equity transferred into another. Microsoft combined the products Word, PowerPoint, Excel, and Outlook into the single product Office, which became a strategic brand. Unilever transferred the equity of Rave hair products to Sauve and Surf detergent products to All.

The fourth step is to implement the strategy. That transition can be made abruptly or gradually. An abrupt transition can signal a change in the overall business and brand strategy; it becomes a one-time chance to provide visibility and credibility to a change affecting customers. So when Norwest Bank acquired Wells Fargo and changed the name Norwest to Wells Fargo, they had the opportunity to communicate new capabilities that would enhance the offering for customers.

When there is a risk of alienating or confusing existing customers, another option is to migrate customers from one brand to another gradually. When Nestle transferred the Contadina brand to their Buitoni label, there was a four-year period in which the Contadina brand was first endorsed by the Della Case Buitoni (from the house of Buitoni) and the imagery of the package was given a Buitoni flavor. That was followed by a year during which Buitoni was endorsed by Contadina before the ultimate change was made.

THE BOTTOM LINE

Brands do not often stand alone. The organization needs to develop a portfolio strategy that creates clarity, synergy, relevance, leverage, and well-defined brand roles, rather than confusion and lost opportunities. In doing so, it is important to understand the brand spectrum and driver roles. Subbrands provide some distance from a master brand, endorsed brands more, and a new brand generates complete separation. The driver role reflects the power of the brand to influence purchase decisions and define use experiences. An optimal brand portfolio depends critically on identifying and resourcing the strategic brands that include current power brands, future power brands, and linchpin brands. The strategist needs to manage the niche, flanker, and cash cow brands, and eliminate the rest from the portfolio using an objective analysis. When the brand team gets the portfolio strategy right, magic can happen. The sum will then be much larger than the parts.

Chapter 18

BRAND EXTENSIONS: THE GOOD, THE BAD, AND THE UGLY

Brands have become the barrier to entry,
but they are also the means to entry.
—Edward Tauber

For nearly three decades, Walt Disney was defined by cartoons such as the Steamboat Willy (Mickey Mouse) series and by animated movies like *Snow White*, *Bambi*, and *Cinderella*. Then, in 1955, arguably one of the most significant brand extensions in history occurred when Disney opened Disneyland and provided hands-on family entertainment leveraging the Disney characters and introducing unique experiences like "Magic Mountain," "It's a Small World," "Tom Sawyer's Island," and much more. At about the same time, the Wonderful World of Disney TV show came to life to support the theme park and the new Disney brand.

The Disney brand became very different from that of a cartoon or animated movie brand and created a rich relationship with its public, delivering nostalgic family experiences. The Disneyland success gave Disney permission to extend into other Disney theme parks, Disney films without animation, Disney stores, a Disney cruise ship, Disney hotels, Disney musicals, Disney TV shows, a Disney TV channel, and more. All of these generated brand-building synergy supporting not only the Disney brand with its brand vision of kids, family, and magic moments, but also with its large and growing family of brands, ranging from Donald Duck to the Lion King to Disneyland itself.

One recipe for strategic success is to create and leverage assets; in fact, that might be the essence of strategy. In most firms one of the most powerful assets is the brand. A brand extension can strengthen and expand a brand while supporting a new offering in another product market thereby providing a growth platform. Extending an established brand is an alternative to the risky and expensive option of creating and establishing a new brand.

Brand extensions like those of Disney can contribute "good" to the new business and also to the brand, but extensions can potentially generate some "bad" and even some "ugly." An analysis of the brand-extension option needs to understand all three.

THE GOOD—THE BRAND ENHANCES THE EXTENSION OFFERING

An established brand name can help a new offering by saving go-to-market time and resources while enhancing the chances of success. It can provide the credibility of an established brand with a history of delivering behind a brand promise and sometimes access to an installed customer base. But its greatest value is often helping to create awareness and helpful associations for the new offering.

Awareness

A very basic task when entering a new product market is simply to become visible. To be considered and thus relevant you need visibility. It is much easier to introduce an established brand such as Disney to a new category such as baby clothing, than it is to build an unknown brand. People just have to learn to connect a known brand to a new category rather than learning a new brand name and connecting it to a category.

Brand Associations

A brand has associations that can help the new offering by providing or supporting a value proposition.

- **Product category relevance**—IBM's experience with computers helped them be a presence in IT Solutions. Starbucks is all about a premium coffee experience, which helped their coffee maker Verismo and the Dreyer's Starbucks Coffee Ice Cream brand. Crest toothpaste provided credibility for Crest toothbrushes.
- **Attribute/functional benefits**—The taste of Hershey's travels, Nyquil's impact on sleep helps tell the Zzzquil story, and Planters Peanut Butter suggests that the peanut ingredient will be the best. Mr. Clean Car Wash has a meaningful symbol behind it.
- **Technological credibility**—Duracell Durabeam flashlights and Duracell Powermat (keeps your smartphone working), both benefit from the battery reputation of Duracell. Tide Dry Cleaners will know cleaning. GE leveraged its turbine technology credibility when it entered the jet engine business.
- **Organizational values**—Kashi, which started in 1984, built a cereal brand around products that emphasized natural ingredients selected for nutritional benefits, such as seven whole grains The brand was extended to snack bars, soft-baked squares, crackers, crisps, pilaf, and even waffles, always demonstrably being the healthiest entry in the category.
- **Brand personality/self-expressive benefits**—The personality and lifestyle of a Caterpillar user affects the image of their line of clothing and footwear. The Virgin personality has worked in a host of categories.

When the brand has associations that are strongly tied to a product class, the extension potential is limited. However, when a brand's equity is based on more abstract associations, it will travel farther. Some core brand associations, such as technological credibility, organizational values, brand personality, user imagery (AXE), style (Calvin Klein), healthy eating (Healthy Choice), and lifestyle (Nike) are not associated with a specific product class and will be capable of casting a wider shadow than a product that is tied to a product-specific attribute.

MORE GOOD—THE EXTENSION ENHANCES THE BRAND

The focus of most extensions is on making sure that it is successful. Yet an equally, or sometimes more important consideration, should be how the extension affects the brand.

Extensions provide visibility and association enhancement for the brand. Giorgio Armani, a big name in the global fashion industry, has ventured into categories like eye wear, watches, cosmetics, and even hotels (Armani Hotel Dubai), up-market furniture (Armani Casa), confectionary (Armani/Doci), and flowers (Armani Flowershop). The Armani name gets a visibility bump every time it is encountered. All this exposure is a bonus for the brand—exposure that would not otherwise occur. And simple exposure also implies market acceptance and capability. Studies have shown that customers are impressed with firms that can cross product classes successfully.

Extensions also provide energy to the brand, a key needed element and one that can drive enhanced visibility, especially when they are successful and involve innovation. Dove, for example, has leveraged its bar soap brand and moisturizer association into body wash with Nutrium, deodorant, cleansing cloths, shampoo with Weightless moisturizers, Nutrium soap, Dove for men, and more. Each successful entry involved visible innovation and provided energy as well as visibility to the Dove brand. The original bar soap saw its sales double as a result of the extension vitality. Tide has similarly leveraged innovation. The very successful Tide Pen provides Tide with an aura of innovation and success.

An extension can expand the scope of the brand and add associations that can be leveraged. When IKEA went into home building, it created another growth platform while also providing the brand with a less confining image. The success of Virgin Airlines completely remade the Virgin brand, which was then connected to an edgy music company. It enabled it to be the flag carrier for over three hundred different businesses including Virgin Money and Virgin Rail.

Finally, extensions can provide a larger budget for marketing and brand-building programs. Big-ticket programs such as sponsorships and event promotions will be more accessible and more cost effective when there is a larger sales base supporting the brand.

THE BAD—THE BRAND FAILS TO HELP OR EVEN INHIBITS THE EXTENSION

A brand's capability of helping an extension depends on the brand strength, but also on its fit and credibility in the new context. If the fit is "off" or credibility is lacking, the brand may hurt instead of help the extension. Consider the following failed extensions, all with some supporting logic:

- Harley-Davidson found that its brand did not work for wine coolers, maybe because bikers are not interested in such a product.
- The Levi Strauss "Tailored Classics" line of suits failed in large part because of Levi's associations with casual living, rugged materials, and the outdoors.
- A taste association was incompatible with the extension offering in the case of Lifesaver Soda (taste like candy), Frito-Lay Lemonade (salty lemonade), and Colgate Kitchen Entrees (toothpaste taste)
- The Swatch car suffered because Swatch's credibility in colorful watches did not transfer to automobiles.
- Bausch & Lomb, the eye care specialist, decided to leverage its R&D, distribution channels, and perceived quality into the mouthwash market and failed—there was no customer benefit.
- Bic Perfume offered convenience and disposability but lacked credibility in the perfume arena.
- Sony and Apple have struggled to extend into the business market and Cisco, IBM, and others have found it difficult to move into the home market, in part because of the brand personality and category competence each has fostered.

The fit issues are not always symmetric. Log Cabin was unable to extend its syrup brand to the pancake mix business; the association with a sticky, sweet syrup probably did not engender visions of a light and fluffy product. In contrast, Aunt Jemima, with links to the friendly Aunt Jemima character, was successful in going the other way—from pancake mix to syrup.

THE UGLY—THE EXTENSION DAMAGES THE BRAND

The brand name is often the key asset of the firm. An ill-advised or poorly implemented extension could damage the brand, especially if the extension did not fail quickly and quietly.

Diluting Existing Brand Associations

The brand associations created by the extension can fuzz a sharp image that had been a key asset, and at the same time reduce the brand's credibility within its original setting. The undisciplined overuse of the Lacoste Alligator and the Gucci brand eroded their image and ability to deliver self-expressive benefits. Recovery for each was slow and expensive.

A distinction should be made between adding and diluting associations. If the original associations are strong, they are unlikely to be affected by an extension that simply adds other associations that do not introduce inconsistencies. When Michelin offers the Michelin Easy Grip Snow Chain, that does not dilute its credibility and relevance with tires.

Undesirable Attribute Associations Get Created

An extension will usually create new brand associations, some of which can be potentially damaging to the brand in its original context. There is certainly a possibility that Sunkist fruit rolls hurt the Sunkist health image, that Black & Decker small appliances hurt the power tool image, that an investment bank image might have suffered when it became part of a retail bank, or that Lipton Soup more than a half century ago hurt the image of a purveyor of fine teas.

Departing from the base brand introduces risks because the brand, instead of being strengthened, made richer, and enabled to do more, can be damaged or even destroyed. Stretching the brand can be risky. The end result will depend on the success of the extensions, the nature of the reframing of the brand, and the ability of the firm to manage the strategy going forward.

The Brand Fails to Live Up to Its Promise

Any extension will risk brand equity if it does not deliver on the key brand promise. That is particularly true if the extension draws on the brand's loyal customer base. When Black & Decker extended its power tool brand into kitchen appliances, a perception that the performance of the appliance line was unreliable or disappointing would potentially affect the image of the Black & Decker power tools because the target market of both overlapped. The brand is particularly vulnerable if the brand is extended vertically downward—that will be the subject of the next chapter.

A negative incident attributed to a brand will be more likely to happen and potentially cause more damage if the brand has been extended to too many categories. The Audi 5000 was accused of having a "sudden acceleration" problem, an accusation that was almost certainly false. As result, the whole Audi line, not just the Audi 5000, was held back for two decades. The threat of a child molestation charge has inhibited Fisher-Price from going into the child-care business because their broad range of children's products could be affected.

FINDING EXTENSION CANDIDATES

If there is a new concept or finished product or service, the question may be whether an existing brand can be extended to provide the needed offering brand. Research that identifies what the brand delivers and receives from the new offering can help make that judgment. The new offering can be evaluated with and without the brand in place. The difference in responses will signal exactly how the brand is adding (or subtracting) value, if at all. The study can go on to determine an impact on the brand for the new offering.

If a new offering concept is not in place, the challenge is to pick a category into which the brand might be leveraged. A four-step process can be employed.

The process starts with a determination of a brand's associations because they are candidates on which to drive an extension concept. A variety of research methods are available to uncover associations and their strength of each. One exercise that can help is to ask respondents to identify from a set of categories several that fit the brand and a few that are bad fits and explain the reasons behind the choice. The strong leverageable associations will usually emerge, as will problem associations. Wells Fargo may have associations such as the stagecoach, Old West, safes, reliability, and entrepreneurial spirit, while McDonalds may be connected to kids, families, Big Mac, Ronald McDonald, McCafe, and more.

The next step is to identify extension product category options. To do so, consider each association and try to think of categories in which it would be relevant and add value. Wells Fargo, for example, might consider extending into home safes or Western clothing and McDonalds into kid's toys or family cruise ships.

Third, the candidate categories then need to be evaluated. Is the category attractive and will it remain so? Is it growing? Are margins healthy? What is the competitive landscape? Does the firm have the assets and resources to compete?

Finally, the potential offering needs to be identified and evaluated. Few "me too" new offerings succeed. We know from dozens of studies of new offerings that meaningful differentiation is the single highest correlate of market success. There should be no illusion that a brand, no matter how strong and relevant, can lead to success in a new category without an offering that is both innovative and has a convincing story. The right brand can only enable an innovative offering with a compelling value proposition; it cannot do more.

Creating Range Brand Platforms

A brand-extension decision usually tends to be ad hoc with a short-term perspective. A more strategic brand strategy should conceive of range brand platforms rather than brand extensions. A range brand spans product classes, leveraging a differentiating association. Dove, for example, has a range brand platform that uses the moisturizer association to create a point of differentiation in a host of extension categories. Strategists should not look at the "next" extension but, rather, consider an ultimate brand vision and the sequence of extensions that will be needed to get there.

In implementing a range brand platform strategy, the sequencing of extensions is managed so that the brand scope is gradually enlarged. Ultimately, extensions that at one point would be an excessive stretch become feasible as the brand evolves into its new portfolio strategy. For example, Gillette meant razors when it introduced Gillette Foamy, a shaving product but not a razor. Gillette Foamy, closely linked to razors, was a bridge to the line of toiletries for men introduced under the Gillette series brand.

Putting Extension Risks into Perspective

There are risks associated with some brand extensions that can fairly be described as so scary that they should be off the table. However, a business case might be so compelling that risks to the brand may be worth taking. There might be strategic upside to having a stretched extension succeed thus opening up new growth options. Ultimately, the brand strategy needs to support the business strategy, not stand in its way.

Further, the risks can be reduced. The use of a subbrand or even an endorsed brand can separate the extension from the master brand, thereby reducing risks due to a performance or fit issue. In addition, the extension can be carefully positioned to reduce any effect of its associations on the master brand. If the associations overlap they should not be presented differently or inconsistently in the extension context.

THE BOTTOM LINE

Extensions can expand a business base and provide new growth platforms. The good—a brand can help a new offering gain visibility and needed associations. The more good—the new offering can enhance the brand's visibility and associations as well as expand the brand's scope and provide a larger budget for brand building. The bad—the brand associations can fail to help or even damage the new offering. The ugly—the new offering can damage the brand by diffusing its image, by creating an undesired association, or by a marketplace blunder or accident. Determining candidate extensions involves finding leverageable brand associations, finding an offering that has a compelling value proposition, and making sure that extension is not ad hoc but part of a larger vision.

Chapter 19

VERTICAL BRAND EXTENSIONS HAVE RISKS AND REWARDS

We've learned that our big brands have broad shoulders.
—**Charles Strauss,** President of Unilever

With the mainstream market of many premium brands turning hostile, with debilitating overcapacity, shrinking markets, and dismal growth prospects, there is business logic to consider entering two emerging niches that are often healthy and growing. One is down-market, the home of value brands. The other is upmarket, where super-premium brands are not only enjoying growth and margins but often buzz as well.

Such a decision means that the new marketplace is judged to be attractive with respect to growth prospects, competitor presence, and margins. It further means that the firm has decided that it has or can obtain the necessary assets and skills to win in the new arena. For the down-market, it means creating a sustainable cost advantage, or at least reaching cost parity with other firms. For the up market, ways need to be found to be credible in the marketplace and be able to create an appealing brand promise.

The risks of using an existing brand to reach these niches are much higher than those found in other extension contexts. It is important to understand those risks and know how they can be managed. Brand strategy does not have the luxury to exist independent of the business strategy. If the business strategy dictates a vertical move, brands need to support.

MOVING INTO A VALUE MARKET

A value market may be a compelling option for a premium brand faced with maturing markets with shrinking margins. There may be several drivers of the growth and vitality of a value market. First, customers may be becoming more price sensitive, perhaps stimulated by economic uncertainty or an impression that a category has become less differentiated, making price a more dominant factor in brand decisions. Second, value retailers such as Amazon, Target, Walmart, Costco, Home Depot, and Office Depot may be the high-growth channels. To participate fully in these channels, a value brand offering may be needed. Third, new disruptive technologies, such as the Crest SpinBrush or GE's portable Vscan ultrasound scanner, make a value offering more relevant or remove a prior disadvantage.

The value space is not only an opportunity for growth; it can be strategically important for other reasons.

- Without the associated sales volume, the firm may lack necessary scale economies. That was one motivation for Mercedes to offer a low-priced A model; their business needed the production volume.
- Competitors with the potential to encroach on the mainstream markets may be getting a foothold. It can be strategically important to blunt their progress with a flanker brand. Intel introduced the Celeron processor with "performance that matches your budget," in part to blunt the progress of competitors like AMD.
- As a market matures and customers become more knowledgeable, they may no longer be willing to pay for advice and services. Xiameter by Dow Corning allowed the firm to provide a "silicon simplified" online offering to serve the growing segment that no longer needed the Dow Corning

service support, impressive though it was and, instead, wanted a lower-priced product.

Branding the Value Entry

How should the value entry be branded?

One option is to create an entirely new stand-alone brand. When Gap developed a value retail chain to reach the lower end of the market, the name Gap Warehouse was found to taint the Gap brand and spawn cannibalization, so they decided to use the Old Navy brand. The problem is that few can afford to develop a new brand, particularly at the value end, where cost considerations prevent supporting a brand-building effort and where it is difficult to create an attention-getting message. Old Navy was blessed with scale and personality that few value players will have.

Another option is to use an existing brand that is owned and redundant. Samsonite used the American Tourister brand to serve the low end of the luggage market and respond to the demands of the discount and mass merchants. GE Appliances had the Hotpoint brand available for use as a value brand. Toyota used the Datsun brand, dormant for some thirty years, to provide a value automobile entry for emerging markets. Such strategy leverages the equity that otherwise would be wasted. However, in most cases, such a brand is not available.

In most contexts, then, a viable entry into the value market will require the use of a premium brand, which involves three types of risks.

First, using an established premium brand to provide visibility and credibility in a value market risks tarnishing the brand. Brand-quality perceptions can be degraded if the value entry lacks or is perceived to lack the quality expected from the brand. TED, the prestige event with polished speakers that stimulate and fascinate, decided to allow a wide selection of groups put on a TED-like event labeled as TEDX. But some of the TEDX presenters, not vetted by TED, were embarrassingly wrong or bad presenters. The TED image was put at risk as a result.

Second, a value entry can create a cannibalization problem, as there have been many occasions when most of the buyers for the value entry came from existing customers of the premium brand. Associating the premium brand with the value offer can reduce the perception that the value brand will be inferior or unreliable, which is why premium brand loyalists have avoided buying "value brands."

Finally, there is the ironic reality that the value offering may fail because customers expect that it may be relatively high-priced, a problem when value is the driver. Customers are looking for value cues and a premium brand can send the wrong signal.

One branding alternative is to abandon the premium market and reposition its brand as a value brand. If the premium brand is struggling in a competitive environment or if it has been tarnished because of a quality incident, such a choice may be a strategically optimal use of the brand. In that case, the first two risks vanish and the third is usually more than compensated by the benefit of the brand's equity. But when the premium brand is an ongoing player in a large, worthwhile market, walking from that position and its sales volume is not wise or even feasible.

Using Subbrands or Endorsed Brands

The risks can be reduced by the use of subbrands or endorsed brands, as suggested by the discussion of the brand spectrum introduced in Chapter 17.

Subbrands, by distinguishing the downscale offering from the parent brand, can reduce the risk of cannibalization and image damage. This job is more feasible when the value offering itself is very distinctive and the subbrand reinforces the difference. When the offering is difficult to distinguish, as in motor oil or detergents, because key product characteristics are not visible, the distinguishing challenge is more severe. In contrast, the MINI Cooper from BMW, the retro-looking, funky, tiny car, is visually and functionally so different from the mainstream BMW line that the risk is reduced. When the differences are less visible, it can be helpful to create different personalities supported by logos, color, and brand-building efforts to provide the necessary separation. The subbrand could be, for example, the fun "kid" in the family in contrast to the "parent" brand.

A subbrand can imply a qualitatively different offering or one that is designed for a different segment. Subbrands like Express or Junior or Mini denote that the offering is in the family but will be limited in some way. Pizza Hut uses the brand Pizza Hut Express for those outlets with limited menus and no table service. Sainsbury, the UK retailer, launched the Sainsbury's Savacentre format, emphasizing the value position. P&G has Bounty Basic and Tide Simply Clean & Fresh to signal value entries.

An endorsed brand provides more separation from the parent brand than does a subbrand. Marriott was able to use an endorsed-brand strategy to help it move into value arenas such as Courtyard by Marriott, Marriott's Fairfield Inn, and Marriott's SpringHill Suites. The brand is then used to provide credibility and visibility to the offering and sometimes functional benefits as well, such as a reservation and reward system in the case of Marriott. But it still involves risks to the brand because it provides visibility to the connection between the parent brand and the value entry, which can lead to both cannibalization and image erosion. Marriott was apprehensive about using its brand on value offerings, but the business logic—that the Marriott brand endorsement was a critical element—was compelling.

MOVING A BRAND UP

Customers and firms are attracted to the very high end of the market because that is where the interest, vitality, and sometimes prestige and self-expressive benefits reside. Brands that are stuck in mature, boring contexts lack not only energy and vitality, but also points of differentiation, and look with envy on the smaller but more attractive upper-end brands. Designer roasted coffee and Starbucks stores, in contrast to canned coffee in the supermarket, have unique features and offerings that touch people's values and lifestyles. Microbreweries, luxury cars, decorator appliances, and green cleaners all are capable of generating interest and injecting energy into tired categories.

The high end also tends to be attractive for financial reasons. It can represent a growth submarket containing high margins. In both developing and developed countries the affluent segment is growing and seeks out the high-end brands. Often the mainstream consumers are increasing their tendency to splurge with indulgent luxuries even when conserving elsewhere. Further, premium pricing and differentiated brands lead to attractive margins. One company had a super-premium lubricant brand that did roughly five percent of sales and made around 90 percent plus of the profits of the business.

One strategic issue is whether the firm has the assets, competencies, innovative offering ideas, marketing power, and commitment to create a super-premium entry that will be accepted. To enter with an offering that is not perceived as having a meaningful value proposition in the upmarket context is a recipe for disappointment, if not failure. Another issue is how should the upmarket offering be branded?

Branding the Upmarket Entry

The first brand option is to create a new brand that does have permission to play at the upper parts of the marketplace and to deliver self-expressive benefits. This option can be expensive and difficult, but was considered necessary when Toyota created Lexus. The firm believed that the Toyota brand, which signaled economy, quality, and functional benefits relevant to the mainstream market, would not support a higher-priced entry based on prestige, handling, and comfort. When Black & Decker created a line of tools for the construction professional, there was no mention of the Black & Decker brand because of its association with the do-it-yourself homeowner and, worse, with kitchen appliances. The DeWalt brand was created with a signature bright yellow, in contrast to the green of the Black & Decker line. Such a strategy still allows brands like Lexus and DeWalt to deliver self-expressive benefits, while people are still comforted by the unspoken fact that Toyota and Black & Decker are behind them as "shadow endorsers."

Another branding option is to identify or acquire an established brand that has credibility in the target upmarket. The Chinese car firm, Geely bought Volvo in part to have a brand that could compete globally in a market segment that was more upmarket than the Geely brand could support.

Using Subbrands and Endorsed Brands

Creating or acquiring a new brand for an upmarket entry can be enormously expensive, difficult, and sometimes simply not feasible. The alternative is to use an existing, established brand with a subbrand or endorsed brand to support the new entry. The use of an existing brand will:

- make the brand-building task more feasible and less costly. Much of the expense of created visibility and associations for a new brand name is reduced or avoided. It is potentially easier to associate Budweiser with a super-premium beer, or GE with an upscale appliance, than to start with a new name that must be established in the midst of marketplace clutter.

- sometimes help provide a value proposition. Thus, customers of GE Profile appliance know that they can access the GE customer service system.
- help the parent brand by associating with it higher quality offerings and the prestige and credibility that goes with them. Gallo has used subbrands to break out of the jug wine category with award-winning entrees such as Gallo Family Vineyards Sonoma Reserve and Gallo Signature Series. It can be a win-win.

There two challenges. First, the brand will often simply lack credibility in that there is no confidence that it can deliver the perceived quality or functional benefits. The organization behind the brand will have been perceived to have made a commitment to a different quality level. Second, the brand may be inconsistent with the need to deliver self-expressive benefits that may be driving the super-premium arena.

Both credibility and self-expressive benefits were missing in the Volkswagen Phaeton, a car that was hoped to compete, indeed surpass, the high-end Mercedes and BMW models. The public simply did not believe that a Volkswagen car could live in that rarified atmosphere. It just did not fit. Coors Extra Gold lager with a deeper color and fuller flavor than other Coors beers became Extra Gold to escape the associations of the Coors brand. Even an endorsement strategy can face the same challenges. The endorsement by Holiday Inn of Crowne Plaza was dropped because it was just too inconsistent with the Crowne Plaza brand position.

A subbrand or endorsed-brand option is more likely to work when the value proposition of the super-premium offering is clear because it is based on something tangible, perhaps protected by a branded differentiator, and is not relying on a subjective self-expressive benefit. Appliances from Siemens by Porsche Designs will have a design edge and P&G's Bounty Dura Towels, positioned to replace germ-filled washcloths, take paper towels up a notch functionally. An upscale describer such as special edition, premium, select, professional, platinum (the Platinum card), or Connoisseur Class (Singapore Air) can help signal an enhanced functional benefit.

A process, ingredient, or technology story behind the brand can provide the missing credibility. Budweiser tells of how their Budweiser Black Crown was created. Twelve world-class brewers engaged in a competition to invent the best lager beer. The winning beer, selected by some 25,000 testers, was a golden-amber lager that used toasted-caramel malt with beachwood aging. The story allowed Black Crown to gain acceptance in the rarified atmosphere of high-end beers despite being a Budweiser brand.

THE BOTTOM LINE

Vertical extensions can have a compelling business rationale, as the value markets often have growth plus scale and the upscale segments deliver growth, margins, and buzz. It is important when pursuing them to make sure that the organization can deliver behind a very different brand promise and to understand the branding options and the associated benefits and risks or each. When a premium brand is used to support a value extension, it risks being tarnished and precipitating cannibalization. When it is used for a super-premium it may lack credibility. The use of subbrands and endorsed brands can reduce the risks.

Chapter 20

SILO ORGANIZATIONS INHIBIT BRAND BUILDING

We have met the enemy and he is us.
—Pogo

D o any of the following branding disaster scenarios, created by organizational silos that do not communicate or cooperate, sound familiar? Do product or country or functional silos in your organization lead to:[1]

Silo-spanning brands that are confused both internally and externally. Too often a master brand, perhaps even a corporate brand, is shared by many product or country silo groups, each motivated to exploit the brand for its own purpose. There is no person or team with any authority that is in charge of the brand. As a result, inconsistent brand positioning and communication strategies damage the brand and result in debilitating marketplace confusion. Having a mixed brand message also makes it hard to convince the organization that the brand stands for something.

A failure to leverage brand-building success across silos. With a multi-silo organization, pockets of marketing or offering brilliance may result that are isolated and not communicated across the organization. The challenge is to recognize and leverage such excellence whenever and wherever it emerges.

A failure to employ brand-building programs that require organization-wide scale. Many potentially effective brand-building programs are not cost-effective for a silo business that lacks the necessary economies of scale. When silo business units are aggregated across products or countries, the economics change. Sponsorships like the World Cup or internal programs like Sephora's BeautyTalk become feasible. Effective brand building also requires functional silos, such as advertising, sponsorship, and digital marketing to become integrated, so that the message is reinforced and amplified. Too often, functional silos compete against each other instead of work together.

The misallocation of brand-building resources. Silos teams are organizationally and psychologically unable to make optimal cross-silo, brand-building resource allocation judgments. The political and economic power of the larger units usually prevails at the expense of smaller units or even proposed business offerings. And white space between product silos does not get accessed at all. What is needed is an objective, credible, organization-wide system of evaluation and resource allocation that will identify and fund brand building in the product markets that represent the largest future potential.

Mishandled cross-silo offerings. Customers are looking for silo-spanning offerings and value propositions. Walmart wants to do business with P&G and not with dozens of product divisions. Citibank wants suppliers that interact globally to avoid country-by-country relationships. There is a need for entertainment systems rather than components, and health care systems rather than ad hoc medical suppliers. To generate such offerings, silos need more than talking; they need to work together.

Weakened marketing and branding competencies. Today marketing needs to draw on specialized skills in multiple areas such as digital marketing, CRM programs, big data, marketing effectiveness modeling, PR, and so on. Further, all needs to be integrated and guided by brand strategies. Efforts to decentralize such functions into silo units will, at best, create redundant staffs that are small, isolated, and ineffective. The solution usually involves centralization or some form of tight coordination.

TOWARD SILO COOPERATION
AND COMMUNICATION

In order to deal with silo-driven problems, firms throughout the world are creating, expanding, or energizing the corporate CMO position and the supporting central marketing group. The task is not easy for sure. Efforts by a CMO team to gain credibility, traction, and influence represent a formidable task in the face of silo indifference or, more likely, resistance.

To determine how to create strong brands and exceptional marketing in a silo world, executives from more than forty companies were interviewed, most of whom were in CMO or comparable positions, and the rest had visibility into the CMO role.[2] They were asked to identify silo-driven problems and what had been done to successfully deal with those problems. A general conclusion—in most contexts, don't blow up the silos because their ability to provide accountability, "close to the market" insights, and decisiveness is valuable. Instead, what is needed is to replace isolation and competition with communication and cooperation—anything that advances that goal will be helpful. Some specifics:

Realize That Non-Threatening Roles
Can Be Powerful Change Agents

The temptation for a new or revitalized CMO is too often to move quickly; to centralize decision making, marketing budgets, and marketing programs that span silos. That strategy may be appropriate when a firm is in crisis and strong CEO support exists for change, but too often it just leads to a flameout.

There are other less threatening CMO roles with reduced risk of failure that can have significant influence by moving an organization toward communication and cooperation by pursuing the non-threatening roles of facilitator, consultant, or service provider. In a facilitator role, the CMO team can establish a common planning framework, foster communication, encourage and enable cooperation, create data and knowledge banks, and upgrade the level of marketing talent throughout the organization. In the consultant role, the CMO would become an invited participant in the silo process, in which brand strategy and marketing programs are developed. As a service provider, the silo business units would "hire" the CMO team to provide marketing services such as marketing research, segmentation studies, training, or consulting on marketing programs such as sponsorships or promotions. These modest roles have had a major impact on strategy, programs, and even on the culture of the organization in many firms.

Use Cross-Silo Organizational Devices Like Teams and Networks

Cross-silo teams with clear goals and effective leaders, such as HP's Customer Experience Council, DowCorning's Global Marketing Excellence Council, or IBM's Global Marketing Board, are powerful devices to stimulate cross-silo information flows, develop synergistic programs, and enable cross-silo relationships.

Formal and informal networks, another key organizational tool, can be based on topics such as customer groups, market trends, customer experience contexts, geographies, or functional areas like sponsorship or digital marketing. Nestle, for example, has developed silo-spanning information networks around global customers such as Tesco or Walmart and interest areas such as the hispanic market and "mom and kids." The network members are motivated to keep in contact with counterparts in other countries to learn of intelligence that could apply to their markets.

Install a Common Marketing Planning Process and Information System

A standardized brand and marketing program, one that is virtually the same across country or product silos, is rarely optimal. What is optimal is to have both a planning process, including templates and frameworks, and a supporting information system that are the same everywhere. Having a common planning process provides the basis for communication by creating a common vocabulary, set of measures, information bank, and decision structure.

Have a Process That Adapts Brands to Silo Contexts

To avoid having a brand that spans silos becoming confused and inconsistent, a best practice organization will have brands that are adapted to silo contexts while still maintaining consistency of the brand character. The adaptation, as explained in Chapter 3, allows for a brand vision to be augmented in a silo context or introduces the flexibility to have a vision element be interpreted or prioritized differently in the silo contexts. Without such an adaptation mechanism, silo groups will recognize that the brand vision and position, determined centrally, will simply not work in their market. Adaptation provides an outlet that allows consistency and synergy to live, while making the brand relevant in a silo market.

Make the Silos Assets Rather Than Barriers

Silos can and should be a vehicle to enhance, rather than detract from, the ability of the organization to develop strong brands and marketing programs. The existence of multiple silos provides a ready-made laboratory to test and refine ideas as part of a systematic test-and-learn program. Perhaps more important, silos can be a source of ideas for breakthrough products or marketing campaigns that can be rolled out across the organization. Nestle's ice cream snack, Dibs, came from the United States and Levi's Dockers' came from South America. As noted in Chapter 10, McDonald's "I'm lovin it" came from Germany, and Pantene's "Hair So Healthy It Shines" came from Taiwan. The key is to empower silos to hit home runs, to identify great marketing when it does occur, and to be able to test the ideas and roll them out expeditiously.

Get CEO/Organizational Support

To make progress, the CMO team needs credibility and buy-in. A key is to obtain visible CEO support, providing authority and resources. One route to getting the CEO on board is to align the role of marketing with that of the CEO's priority agenda. Focus on growth objectives instead of brand extensions, efficiency and cost objectives instead of marketing synergy or scale, and building assets to support strategic initiatives instead of brand-image campaigns. The objective is to reframe marketing as a strategic driver of the business strategy instead of being a tactical management function. The goal is to avoid having the CMO be positioned as another functional area advocate (every slot needs more resources).

Another route to C-Suite support is to use hard numbers in showing the relationship between marketing and financial performance. When the CMO teams can demonstrate an ROI return or its absence, their stature will be enhanced and their image of being soft and lacking analytical skills will at least be reduced. In this era of financial accountability, the C-Suite team is often uncomfortable when performance is not measured.

Credibility also comes from customer knowledge. In fact, that is the ultimate source of influence. The "customer is telling us that..." is a powerful and hard-to-refute argument. When the CMO team has a better grasp of the customer than the silos, or at least has the same level of customer understanding, the discussions can proceed without the "you don't understand this market" overlay. Having firsthand knowledge of a segmentation study, ethnographic research, satisfaction research, or tracking data will create credibility. If the CMO inputs are based on the emergence of a new segment, a new application, a systematic dissatisfaction with the product, or a declining brand, they will be hard to ignore.

TOWARD INTEGRATED MARKETING COMMUNICATION—IMC

In 1972, a Y&R CEO, Ed Ney, announced that the firm would create a team of specialists representing different modalities, such as advertising, PR, direct response, design, and promotion, in order to provide a combined-team approach to a client's communication needs. The effort, supported by acquiring firms, was labeled "the whole egg." For the past four decades, Y&R and others have attempted to deliver the whole egg but have found the process difficult, in large part because the functional silos too often stand in the way.

Functional silos resist becoming part of an integrated marketing communication (IMC) effort because they regard themselves as competitors for resources, each believing that its approach is the most effective brand-building vehicle. There is seldom an open competition for ideas to determine which silo has the truly great idea. Another problem is that the different modalities, such as advertising, sponsorship, and digital, simply do not communicate well, in part because they do not conceptualize the marketplace in the same way, in part because they use a different vocabulary, and in part because they have very different performance measures. Finally, IMC leaders who could provide a strategic, integrating vision are in short supply.

The need for effective IMC has become intensified, especially with the growth of digital. Reliance on mass media as the cornerstone of the communication program has long since passed. In its place is a broad array of media tools. The concept of "media neutral" integrated communication has become more valued and, for many, critical.

The answer for many is a team-based IMC initiative consisting of outside communication firms that involve a set of relevant modalities. The individual members will be selected on the basis of outstanding talent, a team attitude, and the ability to support the task at hand. The team would be charged with creating and implementing a "big idea." It has worked, but it is not as easy as it sounds. An effort by the communication holding company WPP in 1997 to create a new firm called Da Vinci (and later Enfatico) to handle all marketing for Dell lasted fewer than two years because of its unwieldy size, lack of a heritage culture, a change in the marketing executive team at Dell, and disappointing results. But the idea was a response to a real problem, and WPP has since created some thirty teams for brands like Ford, Coors, and Bank of America. Some of these teams, such as Lincoln (Hudson Rouge), MillerCoors (Cavalry), and Colgate (Red Fuse), have their own name, offices, and website.

Another IMC team approach, led by P&G, is centered on the modality that is the core of the program. For Pampers, for example, it could be the website and social marketing, because the driver is the concept of baby care. For another brand it could be sponsorship. But the principal modality does not have to be advertising. The best agency in the modality for P&G is then selected and a team of supporting agencies formed. The team co-leaders will be selected from that agency and from P&G to direct and coordinate. Crucially, compensation will be team-based.

What have we learned from these efforts to create cross-silo IMC teams and others? A lot, actually. We know that the task is difficult to get started, and *really* difficult to keep going over time. Even successful efforts last for years and then fade or spin out of control when one or more of the critical enabling factors weakens or becomes absent. We also know that the chances of success are higher when there is a:

- **CEO mandate with a compelling business rationale for IMC.** CEO support makes the silo barriers shrink.
- **Strong brand strategy driving the effort.** The strategy must be the integrator, and it must be clear and compelling. Google, for example, has a set of ten values that guide all brand building, such as focus on the user (clean, simple interfaces), do one thing really well, and be fast. These values have helped the silo units have common objectives.
- **Strong strategic leader.** The leader should have organizational influence, a strategic perspective, and team leadership skills. At Apple, one of the few firms that has excelled at IMC, the CEO has played that role.
- **Compensation system that is team-based.** Often, that is a radical departure from the norm of many of the participants and is not easy to implement.
- **Team drawn from a single firm.** An IMC team that is drawn from a single firm such as Y&R will share a culture and will not experience any conflict about who owns the client or the revenue. Multiple firms provide the potential of obtaining more "best in class" team members, but generally speaking, teams with multiple firms suffer from organizational stress. That stress is reduced when there is a strong in-house marketing executive and the firms belong to the same communication holding company such as WPP.
- **Great idea from one of the modalities.** Success breeds a supporting culture.

One IMC success story is P&G's "Thank You Mom" campaign that was applied to the Olympic Games in both 2010 and 2012. The campaign's core was a series of video stories of how moms support their kids growing up and then celebrate Olympic victories. The stories had a lot of heart, emotion, tears of joy, and clarity around the role of moms in the success of Olympic athletes. It is easy to empathize with moms who have fed babies, provided lunches, dealt with skinned knees, supported at swim meets, been there for events, and shared in the joy of winning gold at the Olympics. Everyone can relate to the best of a mom's role.

The campaign spanned dozens of brand silos, including Tide/ Ariel, Pantene, Pampers, and Gillette, and was coordinated across a host of media channels and brand-building vehicles as well. A companion in-store worldwide retailer program for five months before the 2012 London games involved four million retailers and raised more than $25 million to support youth sports programs. A Thank You Mom app allowed people to thank their own moms with personalized content in the form of a video and much more. The programs, estimated to have generated $500 million in sales, provided the prestige and energy of being involved in the Olympics, the feel-good aspect of supporting youth sports, and the authenticity and emotion of hear "real moms" stories.

THE BOTTOM LINE

Isolated product, country, and functional silos are no longer a practical option, as they lead to a failure to create consistent brand messaging, leverage successes, scale programs, allocate brand resources optimally, build-cross silo offerings, and develop needed competences. However, that does not mean a race to centralize or standardize. Rather, the goal should be to foster a culture of communication and cooperation rather than isolation and competition. What works is to use non-threatening roles for the CMO team, teams and networks, common processes and systems, ways to adapt the brand vision, silos as a source of ideas, and CEOs to enable difficult organizational compromises. The functional silo problem has become acute with the advent of digital. IMC teams are needed and the ongoing challenge is to learn to make them work.

Epilogue:

TEN BRANDING CHALLENGES

The twenty principles provide concepts and tools to lead to strong brands and business success, and also reflect ten branding challenges facing brand builders in the coming decades. In particular, firms need to do the following:

1. **To treat brands as assets**. The ongoing pressure to deliver short-term financial results, coupled with the fragmentation of media, will tempt organizations to focus on tactics and measurables and neglect the objective of building assets.
2. **Have a compelling vision**. A brand vision needs to be differentiating, resonate with customers, be feasible to implement, work over time in a dynamic marketplace, adaptable to different contexts, and be communicated. The concepts of brand personality, organizational values, a higher purpose, and getting beyond functional events can help but are not easy to employ.
3. **Create new subcategories**. The only way to grow, with rare exceptions, is to develop "must have" innovations that define new subcategories and build barriers to inhibit competitors from gaining relevance. That requires substantial or transformational

192

innovation and a new ability to manage the perceptions of a subcategory so that it wins.

4. **Generate breakthrough brand building.** Exceptional ideas and executions that break out of the clutter are needed to bring the brand vision to life and are more critical than the size of the budget. Good is just not good enough. With control of communication shifting to the customer, it is useful to look toward customer's sweet spots rather than promoting the brand or the firm, but that is not easy.

5. **Achieve integrated marketing communication (IMC).** IMC is more elusive and difficult than ever because the various modalities, such as advertising, sponsorships, and digital, tend to compete rather than reinforce; because the media scene and options have become so complex; because the marketplace is so dynamic; and because product and country silos reflect competition and isolation rather than cooperation and communication.

6. **Sort out a digital strategy.** This arena is complex, dynamic, and in need of a different mindset because of the audience-in-control reality of much of it. New capabilities, creative initiatives, and ways to work with other marketing modalities are required.

7. **Build the brand internally.** It is hard to achieve IMC or breakthrough marketing without employees both knowing the vision *and caring* about it. The brand vision that lacks a higher purpose will find the inspiration task more difficult.

8. **Maintain brand relevance.** Brands face three threats—fewer customers buying what the brand is offering, emerging reasons not-to-buy, and losing energy. Detecting and responding to each requires an in-depth knowledge of the market, plus a willingness to invest and change.

9. **Create a brand-portfolio strategy yielding synergy and clarity.** Brands need well-defined roles and visions that support those roles. Strategic brands should be identified and resourced, and branded differentiators and energizers should be created and managed.

10. **Leverage brand assets to enable growth.** A brand portfolio should foster growth by enabling new offerings, or extending the brand vertically or into another product class. The goal is to apply the brand to new contexts, where the brand both adds value and is itself enhanced.

ENDNOTES

Chapter 2

[1] A more complete description of the Schlitz debacle is found in David Aaker, *Managing Brand Equity*, New York: The Free Press, 1991, pp. 78-85.

[2] Personal communication from the Interbrand brand valuation group. The 2013 brand values are published on Interbrand.com.

[3] "The Financial Information Content of Perceived Quality" (with Bob Jacobson), *Journal of Marketing Research*, May 1994, pp. 191-201, and "The Value Relevance of Brand Attitude in High Technology Markets," *Journal of Marketing Research*, (with Bob Jacobson) November 2001, pp. 485-493.

[4] This quote appeared as an endorsement to Aaker, *Managing Brand Equity*.

[5] Robert D. Buzzell, "Predicting Short-Term Changes in Market Share as a Function of Advertising Strategy," *Journal of Marketing Research*, August 1964, pp. 27-31.

Chapter 3

[1] The brand-vision model, then termed a brand identity model and sometimes called the Aaker model, was first explicated in David Aaker, *Building Strong Brands*, New York: The FreePress, 1996. It was refined to include a brand essence in David Aaker and Erich Joachimsthaler, *Brand Leadership*, New York: The Free Press, 2000.

[2] The Berkeley-Haas core identity can be found in its website under Defining Principles in the Culture section and also in their "brand card."

Chapter 4

[1] Grainne M. Fitzsimons, Tanya L. Chartrand, and Gavan J. Fitzsimons, "Automatic Effects of Brand Exposure on Motivated Behavior: How Apple Makes You 'Think Different,'" *Journal of Consumer Research*, June 2008, pp. 21-35.

[2] Susan Fournier, "Consumers and Their Brands: Developing Relationship Theory in Consumer Research," *Journal of Consumer Research*, March 1998, pp. 343-353.

[3] Jennifer L. Aaker, "Dimensions of Brand Personality," *Journal of Marketing Research*, August 1997, pp. 347-356.

[4] Jennifer L. Aaker, Veronica Benet-Martinez ,and Jordi Garolera, "Consumption Symbols as Carriers of Culture: a Study of Japanese and Spanish Brand Personality Constructs," *Journal of Personality and Social Psychology*, 81 (3) 2001, pp. 492-508.

Chapter 5

[1] David Aaker and Kevin Lane Keller, "The Impact of Corporate Marketing on a Company's Brand Extensions," *Corporate Reputation Review*, July 1998, pp. 356-378.

[2] From the Uniliver web site, 2013, see sustainable living.

[3] Taken from BrandJapan data, which is based on an annual survey of the brand equity of over one thousand Japanese brands.

Chapter 6

[1] Dan Ariely, *Predictably Irrational*, New York: HarperCollins Publishers, 2008.

[2] Stuart Agres, Emotion in Advertising: An Agency's View, in Stuart J. Agres, Julie A. Edell, and Tony M. Dubitsky, *Emotion in Advertising*, New York: Quorum, 1990, pp. 1-18.

Chapter 7

[1] More a more detailed discussion of the "must have" concept and how it can be implemented see David Aaker, *Brand Relevance: Making Competitors Irrelevant*, San Francisco: Jossey-Bass, 2011.

[2] For a more complete exposition of this study, see Aaker, *Brand Relevance*, pp. 1-5.

[3] W. Chan Kim and Renee Mauborgne, *Blue Ocean Strategy*, Boston: Harvard Business School Press, 2005.

[4] Eddie Yoon and Linda Deeken, "Why It Pays to Be a Category Creator," *Harvard Business Review*, March 2013, pp. 21-23.

Chapter 8

[1] Gregory S. Carpenter, Rashi Glazer, and Kent Nakamoto. "Meaningful Brands from Meaningless Differentiation: The Dependence on Irrelevant Attributes, *Journal of Marketing Research*, August 1994, pp. 339-350.

Chapter 9

[1] George Lakoff, *Don't Think of an Elephant,"* White River Junction, Vermont: Chelsea Green, 2004.

[2] Dan Ariely, *Predictably Irrational*, New York: Harper Books, 2008, pp. 162-163.

[3] Brian Wansick, *Mindless Eating*, New York: Bantam Books, 2006, pp. 19-23.

[4] I. P. Levin and G. J. Gaerth, "Framing of Attribute Information Before and After Consuming a Product," *Journal of Consumer Research,* March 1988, pp. 374-378.

[5] Mita Sujan, "Consumer Knowledge: Effects on Evaluation Strategies Mediating Consumer Judgments," *Journal of Consumer Research*, June 1984, pp. 31-46.

[6] Aaker, Jennifer, Kathleen Vohs and Cassie Mogilner, "Non-Profit Are Seen as Warm and For-Profits as Competent: Firm Stereotypes Matter" *Journal of Consumer Research,* 37, August 2010, pp. 277-291.

[7] Srinivas Reddy and Christopher Dula, "Gillette's 'Shave India Movement,'" *FT.com/management*, November 4 2013.

Chapter 10

[1] This touchpoint process model is taken from Scott M. Davis and Michael Dunn, *Building the Brand Driven Business*, San Francisco: Jossey-Bass, 2002

[2] Emma K. Macdonald, Hugh N. Wilson, and Umut Konus, "A New Tool Radically Improves Marketing Research, *Harvard Business Review*, September 2012, pp. 103-108.

³ Alex Rawson, Ewan Duncan, and Conor Jones, "The Truth About Customer Experience," *Harvard Business Review*, September 2013, pp. 90-99

⁴ G. Lafley and Ram Charan, *The Game-Changer*, New York: Crown Business, 2008, pp. 39-40.

⁵ Richard J. Harrington and Anthony, K. Tjan, "Transforming Strategy One Customer at a Time," *Harvard Business Review*, March 2008, 62-72.

Chapter 11

¹ Adapted from David Aaker, "Find the Shared Interest: A Route to Community Activation and Brand Building," *Journal of Brand Strategy*, Summer 2013, pp. 136-147. The material was also included in David Aaker, *Strategic Market Management* 10 ed., New York: John Wiley, 2014.

² Susan Fournier did pioneering work in the personal relationship metaphor and her thinking is represented in numerous articles and books. See Susan Fournier, Michael Breazeale, and Marc Fetscherin, *Consumer-Brand Relationships*, Abingdon, UK: Routledge, 2013.

Chapter 12

¹ A survey by Nielsen of 29,000 internet users in 58 countries reported that 69 percent of respondents trusted website content and online comments vs. 61 percent for media advertising. The trust level goes up to 84 percent if the opinions come from trusted friends or families. Aaron Baar, "Nielsen: Consumers Trust WOM Over Other Messaging," *Marketing Daily*, September 17 2013.

² Patrick Spenner and Karen Freeman, "Keep It Simple," *Harvard Business Review*, May 2012 pp. 109-114.

³ Thales Teixeira, "Online Video Offers a Way to Achieve Higher Engagement with Consumers for Far Less Money," *Harvard Business Review*, June 2013, pp. 23-25.

⁴ Joe Tripodi, "Coca-Cola Marketing Shifts from Impressions to Expressions," blogs.hbr.org, April 27, 2011.

Chapter 13

¹ Joe Tripodi, "Open Coke," *The HUB*, July-August 2011, pp. 26-30.
Chapter 14

[1] J. Gromark, and F. Melin, "Brand Orientation Index—A Research Project on Brand Orientation and Profitability" in Sweden's 500 Largest Companies, reported in Nicholas Ind, *Living the Brand* 3rd. ed., London: KoganPage, 2007, pp. 66.

Chapter 15
[1] See David Aaker, *Three Threats to Brand Relevance: Strategies that Work*, San Francisco: Jossey-Bass, 2013.
[2] Personal communication from John Gerzema who noted that in 2008 Walmart was ranked number 12 on the social responsibility scale among 3,000 brands tracked by the Young & Rubicam's BrandAsset Valuator database.
[3] Andrew S. Ross, "Green Project Making It Harder to Hate Walmart," *San Francisco Chronicle*, February 28 2010.

Chapter 16
[1] John Gerzema and Ed Lebar, *The Brand Bubble,* San Francisco: Jossey-Bass, 2008, Chapter 2.
[2] Natalie Mizik and Robert Jacobson. The Financial Value Impact of Perceptual Brand Attributes, *Journal of Marketing Research*, February 2008.

Chapter 17
[1] For more detail on the material in this chapter and the two that follow, see David Aaker, *Brand Portfolio Strategy*, New York: The Free Press, 2004.

Chapter 20
[1] For more on the silo problems and their solutions, see David Aaker, *Spanning Silos: The New CMO Imperative*, Boston: Harvard Business Press, 2008.
[2] The study and results are described in detail in Aaker, *Spanning Silos*.

ACKNOWLEDGEMENTS

This book is a product of two and a half decades of working with brands and brand building. During that time I have worked with and been influenced by a lot of smart people. I will mention a few to illustrate but there are many more as well. Among the academics are Jennifer Aaker, Toshi Akustu, Roberto Alvarez, George Day, Susan Fournier, Bob Jacobson, Erich Joachimsthaler, Jean-Noel Kapferer, Kevin Keller, Rich Lyons, and Doug Stayman. Practitioners include people like Stuart Agris, Don Bruzzone, Katy Choi, Ted Hirose and others on the Dentsu team, Jerry Lee, Larry Light, Jim Stengel, Joe Tripodi, Peter Sealey, and Bill Wells.

Many of my ideas have come from or been nurtured by my colleagues at Prophet, the global brand and marketing consulting firm with which I have been associated since 1999. I thank CEO Michael Dun for his support and friendship and Scott Davis, Andy Pierce, and Rune Gustafson for their inspiration. Paul Wang, Scott Drummond, Kurk Texter, and Nick Watts helped create the cover and graphics. Amanda Nizzere was my partner in marketing the book with the support of John Baglio. Ryland Devero and Karen Woon both helped me with my talks and blogging that provided content and energy to the project.

I have been delighted with my partners at Morgan-James, who replace stress in the process with confidence, creativity, and fun. David Hancock is knowledgeable, insightful, and supportive, and has been such a pleasure to work with. Rick Fishman and Jim Howard added helpful advice at critical times. Lyza Poulin coordinated with a relentlessly cheerful, positive style. My copy editor, Lisa Zuniga, elevated the book for sure.

Finally I would like to thank my family—my wife Kay and our daughters Jennifer, Jan, and Jolyn—who continuously support and inspire, and their families who enrich my life.

ABOUT THE AUTHOR

David Aaker, the Vice-Chairman of Prophet Brand Strategy and Professor Emeritus of Marketing Strategy at the Berkeley-Haas School of Business, is the winner of three career awards for contributions to the science of marketing (Paul D. Converse Award), marketing strategy (Vijay Mahajan Award), and the theory and practice of marketing (Buck Weaver Award). He has published more than on hundred articles and seventeen books that have sold well over one million copies and been translated into eighteen languages. They include *Managing Brand Equity*, *Building Strong Brands*, *Brand Leadership* (co-authored with Erich Joachimsthaler) *Brand Portfolio Strategy*, *From Fargo to the World of Brands*, *Spanning Silos*, *Strategic Market Management 10th edition*, *Brand Relevance: Making Competitors Irrelevant* which was named to three best book lists for 2011, and *Three Threats to Brand Relevance*. Named as one of the top five most important marketing/business gurus in 2007, Professor Aaker has won awards for the best article in the California Management Review and (twice) in the Journal of Marketing. A recognized authority on brand strategy, he has been an active consultant and speaker throughout the world. A columnist for AMA's Marketing News and Germany's absatzwirtschaft, he regularly blogs at davidaaker.com and HBR.org. He is at twitter.com/davidaaker. An avid biker and struggling golfer, he lives in Orinda California.

INDEX